核心素养下
高中英语写作的教与学

童莉玲　著

序
FOREWORD

随着全国基础教育改革的不断深入,"以学生发展为本"的课程理念逐渐深入人心。《普通高中英语课程标准(2017 年版 2020 年修订)》明确指出,普通高中英语课程的具体目标是培养和发展学生在接受高中英语教育后应具备的语言能力、文化意识、思维品质、学习能力等学科核心素养。如何在英语教学中培养出顺应时代需求的人才?如何将培养学生学科核心素养的要求真正落实到课堂教学中?这些都是每一位一线教师需要深入思考的问题。

基于对课改背景和上述问题的思考,上海市川沙中学的童莉玲老师结合自己多年的教学经验,撰写了《核心素养下高中英语写作的教与学》一书。该书从一位长期在一线工作的教师的视角出发,对高中英语写作的要求、方法和技巧等进行了全面的梳理和总结。

本书共分为五章,分别是"学生指导""教师指导""教学评价""写作教学的课堂案例""范文参考"。书名中的三个关键词——"核心素养""教""学",清晰地展现了作者的编写意图。

首先,本书对于如何将英语学科核心素养切实落实到课堂教学中,进行了系统性的深度探讨,并提供了许多切实可行的培养路径、方法和策略。

其次,本书针对日常写作教学中经常遇到的问题,从"教师"和"学生"两个不同的视角出发,提供了许多实用的教学方法和学习策略,并辅以丰富的教学案例和写作案例。无论是教师还是学生,都能从本书中获取宝贵的写作经验和实践素材。

再次,值得一提的是,本书的第三章"教学评价",专门探讨了"写作教、学、评一体化”的实施策略。在传统的写作教学中，教师往往更侧重教学生“如何学”，而学的效果往往仅通过作文批改分数或考试结果来衡量。然而，评价是写作教学中不可或缺的重要环节。本书用一整章的篇幅，系统阐述了如何在整个写作教学过程中体现过程性评价和形成性评价，最终实现“以评促教”和“以评促学”的目的，从而提升写作教学的有效性。

本书的最后一部分提供了若干完整的案例分析、范文及点评，为我们的作文教学提供了丰富的参考素材。

总之，这是一本系统、全面探讨如何将英语学科核心素养落实到课堂实践中的书。相信通过深入阅读本书，学生能够获得写作技巧与方法，从而提升英语写作水平；同时，教师也能够从中汲取宝贵的经验，进一步提升自己的教学水平。

2024 年 4 月

前言
PREFACE

高中英语写作是高中英语教学中非常重要的部分，它不仅占据了上海英语高考卷25分的分值，而且对学生的英语学习和综合素质的提升也具有至关重要的作用，具体表现在以下几个方面：

一、高中英语写作有助于培养学生的语言能力。在英语写作过程中，学生需要运用所学的词汇、句型、语法等语言知识，进行思维的整理和表达，从而提高语言运用能力。通过大量的练习与实践，学生可以更熟练地运用英语进行写作，从而全面提升书面甚至口头表达能力。

二、高中英语写作能够培养学生的逻辑思维、批判性思维和创新性思维等思维能力。写作是一个需要进行逻辑和创新性思考的过程。学生在撰写英语作文的过程中，需要发散思维，收集、整理合理的论据，并通过适当的组织结构表达出来。在这个过程中，学生的思维能力会得到锻炼和提升，这是培养英语学科核心素养的重要方面。

三、高中英语写作还能提高学生的文化素养和跨文化交际能力。通过写作，学生能够学习和了解英语国家的文化背景、社会习俗、传统价值观等；同时，写作也是一种跨文化交流的方式，学生可以通过写作与来自不同国家或地区的人进行交流和沟通，了解不同文化之间的差异和相通之处。

四、高中英语写作还能提高学生的综合素质。在写作的过程中，学生需要进行大量的信息查找、整理和归纳工作，这可以帮助他们在获取更多知识的同时，提高他们的信息处理能力；通过写作，学生可以学会发现问题、分析问题、解决问题；同时，写作能锻炼学生的时间管理和组织能力。这些能力对他们日后的学习和工作也是非常重要的。

总之,高中英语写作在学习中具有重要的意义。它不仅有助于培养学生的语言能力、思维能力、表达能力等,而且能提高学生的文化素养和跨文化交际能力,还能提高他们的综合素质。

然而,由于高考对学生写作内容的翔实性、语言表达的多样性、思维的逻辑性和严谨性等提出了较高要求,这让许多英语教师对写作教学感到头疼。本书以学生和教师为主体,从理论和实践两方面出发,指导学生如何学好英语写作、教师如何教好英语写作。

本书的第一章为学生指导,主要从学生的角度入手,按照写作过程为他们提供如何写好一篇英语作文的指导。这一部分将从审题、谋篇布局、段落处理、写作方法、句型结构、语言和思维等多个方面进行探讨。审题是写作过程中至关重要的一步,它决定了写作的方向和内容,我们将介绍如何"破题",即如何正确理解和分析题目,以及如何在作文中明确表达自己的观点和立场。段落处理是写作中组织结构的关键,我们将讨论如何合理划分段落、如何写好主旨句(thesis statement/main idea)和主题句(topic sentence)等。句型结构和语言的运用是写作技巧的体现,我们将分享一些常用的句型和表达方式,帮助学生提高写作的表达能力。此外,我们还会介绍如何培养良好的写作思维、如何拓展思路和丰富内容,以使作文更富有深度和思想性。

第二章为教师指导,主要为教师提供教学方法和技巧,使他们能够有效地教授学生如何写好高中英语作文。教师在教学过程中的指导和启发,对学生的写作学习至关重要。我们将分享一些教学经验和实用技巧,如怎样激发学生的写作兴趣、如何引导学生进行思考和创作,以及如何提供具体的写作指导和反馈,等等。通过这些方法和技巧,教师将能够更好地开展写作教学,激发学生的写作潜力,提高学生的英语写作水平。

第三章为教学评价,对《普通高中英语课程标准(2017 年版 2020 年修订)》提出的教、学、评一体化的教学模式进行理论研究和实践探索。这部分将重点探讨如何运用好作文的评价体系和评价方式来推动作文教学,同时也会介绍如何设计合理的作文评价标准和评价方法、如何根据学生的写作表现进行评价和反馈等内容。评价是教学中不可或缺的一环,它能够激发学生的学习兴趣和动力,促使他们不断提升自己的写作能力。

第四章为写作教学的课堂案例。通过对论文中具体的案例分析,学生和教师能够更好地理解和应用前面所学的写作知识和技巧。这些案例涉及不同文体和不同难度的写作任务、学生在写作过程中可能遇到的问题和解决方法,以及不同文体的作文的教学方式,等等。教师可以通过研读论文和研究案例,提高英语写作教学水平。

第五章收录了不同文体的优秀习作以及教师点评。学生可以通过阅读优秀作文得到启发,了解写作的成功要素和技巧。教师点评对这些优秀习作进行具体分析,以助力学生借鉴和参考。

相信通过这五章内容的学习和实践,学生的英语写作学习能力和教师的写作教学成效将会得到很大的提升。最后,衷心希望:英语写作不再是令人头疼的作业或任务,而是教师展示教学艺术和素养、学生展现思想和表达能力的舞台。

童莉玲

2024 年 4 月

目录
CONTENTS

CHAPTER 01

第一章　学生指导

第一节　写作过程

高中英语写作对学生的语言、思维等各方面的能力提出了非常高的要求，要写出一篇优秀作文，不可能一蹴而就。本章将针对在写作过程中如何审题、如何谋篇布局、如何写好首段和尾段以及如何写好主旨句等问题提供理论依据，并通过写作实践给予具体指导。

一、如何审题

审题是英语写作的重要步骤，它有助于我们更好地理解题目要求、明确写作目的，并将读者意识融入文章。在审题时，我们需做到以下几点：

(一) 仔细阅读题目，理解题目要求

在阅读题目时，我们可以圈画关键词，思考关键信息之间的关系。关键词通常包括主题、时间、地点、人物等等。通过理解关键词，我们可以确定文章的体裁，还可以把握整体方向，确保后续写作不偏离主题。

(二) 分析写作目的

写作目的是指通过写作想要达到的目标，即通过这篇文章想要传达什么信息，或者表达什么观点。写作目的可以是说服、解释、讨论、描述等等。确定写作目的有助于我们在写作过程中有一个明确的方向，并帮助我们更好地组织文章结构。

(三) 建立读者意识

读者意识是指作者在写作过程中对读者的信息需求的关注。不了解读者的信息需求将会导致写作目的无法实现。从读者的角度出发安排写作内容、选择适当的语言进行表达，是实现有效写作的必要手段。建立读者意识，有助于我们使用合适的语言和论据来与读者建立联系，提高文章的可读性和说服力。

下面通过两个写作实践案例，来探讨如何审题。

2017 年上海秋考作文

假设你是明启中学的学生王磊，你校学生会将组织一次徒步活动，并在校园网公布了如下方案，征求师生意见。写一封邮件给活动组织者，内容须包括：

1. 你认为方案中需要改进的地方及改进建议；
2. 你的理由。

活 动 方 案

主题：发现上海
时间：5 月 1 日(星期日)下午 3:00
路线：从人民广场出发，途经南京东路，抵达外滩(the Bund)后原路返回

审题步骤：

1. 仔细阅读题目，理解题目要求

在阅读题目时，我们应关注到以下关键词：

- 关系：作者——学生王磊；书信对象——明启中学学生会
- 目的：征求师生意见
- 主题：发现上海
- 时间：5 月 1 日(星期日)下午 3:00
- 路线：从人民广场出发，途经南京东路，抵达外滩(the Bund)后原路返回

2. 分析写作目的

通过以上关键词，可以得出写作目的为：

- 通过写一封建议信，提出方案中需要改进的地方及改进建议
- 提供这样改进的理由

因此，我们可以得出以下可选结构方案：

- 开头：事由+写信意图

- 展开：
  - 建议＋理由
  - 建议＋理由
  - 建议＋理由（可选）
- 结尾：希望改进建议被采纳

3. 建立读者意识

在审题过程中，我们需要考虑读者即活动组织者的立场和期望。他们希望收到的邮件内容应包括对原方案的批评与建议，同时需要充分的、有说服力的理由来支撑观点，以供活动组织者参考。读者意识很重要的一点是，需体现所采用的语言的风格。该信的读者为学生会，因此文章的措辞可以直白些，这与写给师长的邮件有所不同。

黄浦区 2023 届高三一模作文

假设你是明启中学学生李华，学校正在征求学生对云课堂的感受和建议。请发送一封邮件至校长信箱，你的邮件内容须包括：

1. 详细描述一节云课堂以及你的感受；
2. 简单阐述你对云课堂的态度和建议。

通过审题，我们不难发现：上篇作文是写给学生会的建议信，而本篇是写给校长的建议信，因此文章的语言应该正式，语气更为婉转、客气才比较妥当。

综上所述，审好题是写出优秀作文的前提条件。仔细阅读题目，理解题目要求；分析写作目的；建立读者意识：这些是我们审题的要素。只有充分考虑到这些要素，我们才能更有效地开展英语写作。

二、如何谋篇布局

谋篇布局是英语写作的一个重要环节，它不仅能使文章的结构更加清晰，还能培养和提升我们的英语学科核心素养。

谋篇布局能帮助我们构建一个清晰的框架。只有对全文的组织结构有了一个宏观和全局性的规划，我们才能在落笔时做到心中有数。

下面以高中英语写作中常见的议论文和说明文为例，谈谈如何来进行英语写作的谋篇布局。

(一) 议论文

我们可以将议论文分成导入(Introduction)、主体论证(Body)和结论(Conclusion)三个部分。导入部分引入主题并激发读者的兴趣或提出问题，主体论证部分对主题进行深入的阐述和论证，结论部分总结全文并得出结论。这样的框架能够使整篇文章逻辑清晰、条理分明。

在高中英语写作中，可以采用“四段式”或“五段式”的写作结构。

Title of the Essay

Introduction {background information (to arouse readers' interest) / thesis statement/main idea}

Body {
topic sentence 1 (supporting sentence 1)
    examples and details
topic sentence 2 (supporting sentence 2)
    examples and details
}

Conclusion

图 1 四段式

图 1 的“四段式”是常见的文章结构：在首段中，我们可以阐述背景信息等内容，以此来吸引读者的注意力；第二、第三段展开两个分论点；最后一段则为总结。

Title of the Essay

Introduction {background information (to arouse readers' interest) / thesis statement/main idea}

Body {
topic sentence 1 (supporting sentence 1)
    examples and details
topic sentence 2 (supporting sentence 2)
    examples and details
topic sentence 3 (supporting sentence 3)
    examples and details
}

Conclusion

图 2 五段式 1

Title of the Essay

Introduction { background information (to arouse readers' interest)（独立成段）
thesis statement/main idea（独立成段）

Body { topic sentence 1 (supporting sentence 1)
examples and details
topic sentence 2 (supporting sentence 2)
examples and details

Conclusion

图 3　五段式 2

图 2 和图 3 为"五段式"结构。图 2 中的主体论证部分在"四段式"结构的基础上加了分论点 3，使得文章内容更为翔实。图 3 则把首段的主旨句(thesis statement/main idea)独立成段，使得文章主旨清晰可见。当然，一篇优秀的作文不一定要照搬框架，应根据具体情况来构建文章的结构。

写作实践

现在高中生申请出国留学的现象非常普遍，人们对此看法不一。请谈谈你对此事的看法。

学生习作：

Nowadays, it's quite common for high school students to apply for admission to foreign universities.【开门见山，直截了当描述现象】This trend has sparked heated discussions among students, and people's views towards it vary from individual to individual.【此句可用于多种场合，用来引出人们对某现象的不同认识】Some are in favor of this practice, believing it broadens their horizons, while others are strongly opposed to it, arguing that it's a waste of money. As far as I am concerned, there are both merits and demerits lying in the debatable problem.

On the one hand, studying abroad can be very expensive, often beyond the reach of ordinary families. Many parents may find it difficult to cover all the

expenses. Worse still, without their parents around, some students may lack self-discipline. They may be easily tempted to get into bad habits and ultimately fail to achieve their goals.

On the other hand, we cannot ignore the benefits of studying abroad. It helps cultivate children's independence and social skills. To plus, being exposed to a different culture and environment will definitely enrich their experiences, which will have a far-reaching effect on their future development.【从正反两面阐述现象的两面性,使得内容更加翔实】

As the saying goes, each coin has two sides. Therefore, there's no need to get caught up in the argument.【这句话可以用于任何有争议的话题的总结部分】What we should bear in mind is that wherever we study, we should make the most of the resources available and strive to be responsible learners.【以号召式结尾总结全文,避免与开头重复,又与文章主题切合】

点评

这是一篇典型的现象类文章,即针对一个现象发表自己的观点。整篇文章为典型的"四段式"结构:

段① 导入现象+表明自己的观点(即文章的主旨)

段② 阐述弊端

段③ 阐述优点

段④ 总结

我们可以尝试把文章变成"五段式"结构,即把文章的首段分成如下两段:

首段:导入现象+表明自己的观点(即文章的主旨)——
- 导入现象(独立成段)
- 表明自己的观点(即文章的主旨)(独立成段)

首段修改后:

Nowadays, it's quite common for high school students to apply for admission to foreign universities. This trend has sparked heated discussions among students, and people's views towards it vary from individual to individual. Some are in favor of this practice, believing it broadens their horizons, while others are strongly opposed to it, arguing that it's a waste of money.【导入现象】

As far as I am concerned, there are both merits and demerits lying in the debatable problem.【表明自己的观点,即文章的主旨】

点评

这样处理首段后,一方面使得主旨鲜明突出,另一方面在段落的分配上充分体现了详略得当,使得文章条理更为清晰、更有层次。

(二) 说明文

在高中英语说明文的写作中,最常见的为现象类或问题类作文,其典型的结构为:

介绍(Introduction)	第一段(Para.1)	现象/问题(phenomenon/problem)
正文(Body)	第二段(Para.2) 第三段(Para.3) 第四段(Para.4)	原因(cause) 结果(effect) 措施/建议(measures/suggestions)
总结(Conclusion)	第五段(Para.5)	结论

无论是议论文还是说明文的写作,建议采用"四段式"或更好的"五段式"结构,这样能使得文章结构更为清晰,条理更为有序,内容更富有层次感,也更能做到高分作文所要求的详略得当。

英语写作的谋篇布局非常有助于培养和提升学生的英语学科核心素养。《普通高中英语课程标准(2017 年版 2020 年修订)》明确指出核心素养的重要性:学科核心素养是学科育人价值的集中体现,是学生通过学科学习而逐步形成的正确价值观、必备品格和关键能力。英语学科核心素养主要包括语言能力、文化意识、思维品质和学习能力。这些素养旨在培养学生综合运用英语

语言的能力，促进学生的终身发展和社会适应能力的提升。在谋篇布局时，我们需要运用自主学习的能力进行思考和分析，运用批判性思维对观点进行评估和论证，同时发挥沟通、表达的能力，将自己的想法清晰地传达给读者。通过展现这些核心素养，使得文章不仅在结构上有条理，而且在思维和表达上富有深度和逻辑性。

总之，谋篇布局是英语写作过程中不可或缺的一环，它能够帮助我们构建清晰的框架、合理安排写作内容，并培养和提升核心素养。通过合理的布局，能够提高作文的质量，使文章更具说服力和可读性。因此，掌握谋篇布局的技巧，对于提升英语写作能力和核心素养是非常重要的。

三、如何写好首段和尾段

(一) 首段

高考英语作文字数要求在 120—150 之间，这就要求我们在首段的处理上要言简意赅，开门见山。

首段的基本结构为：背景信息＋文章主旨。导入话题或问题，提供背景信息，并说明这个话题或问题是重要的或值得关注的，继而引出观点或立场；用一两句话概括文章的主要观点，即文章的主旨。

写作实践

现在高中生申请出国留学的现象非常普遍，人们对此看法不一。请谈谈你对此事的看法。

学生习作(首段)：

Nowadays, it's quite common for high school students to apply for admission to foreign universities.【导入话题】This trend has sparked heated discussions among students, and people's views towards it vary from individual to individual. Some are in favor of this practice, believing it broadens their horizons, while others are strongly opposed to it, arguing that it's a waste of money.【人们看法不一，属于背景信息】

As far as I am concerned, there are both merits and demerits lying in the debatable problem.【引出自己的观点，即文章的主旨】

点评

首段可以拆分成两小段，即文章的主旨独立成段，使得观点更为鲜明，读者更容易理解。

作为全文的引领，一个引人入胜、主旨清晰的作文首段，意味着整篇文章成功了一半。因此，首段的写作需要我们重视和多多练习。

(二) 尾段

写好英语作文的尾段也非常关键，好的结尾可以给读者留下深刻的印象。它的基本结构为总结全文的主要观点并给出合适的结论。下面介绍一些写好英语作文尾段的技巧和方法。

1. 总结上文或重申主旨：回顾全文的主要观点和支撑论据，简要概括自己的想法；也可重申主旨，确保尾段与文章主题紧密相关。

写作实践

My Favourite Activities

① My life is full of colourful activities. ② They can bring me joy, help me relax, and contribute positively to my overall well-being.

1. Reading

Reading is one of my favourite activities as it allows me to explore new worlds, gain knowledge, and expand my imagination ...

2. Painting

Painting is another activity that brings me immense joy. It provides a creative outlet for self-expression and allows me to convey my emotions and thoughts onto the canvas ...

3. Playing the guitar

Playing the guitar is not only a hobby but also a way for me to unwind. It allows me to express myself musically and connect with others through music ...

...

① In conclusion, reading, painting, playing the guitar, exercising, and cooking are my favourite activities. ② These activities provide me with relaxation, self-expression, enjoyment, and personal growth. ③ Engaging in these activities enables me to find joy and balance in life, contributing positively to my overall well-being.

点评

尾段①是对上文提到的几个活动的总结,和首段①呼应;尾段的②③重申了文章的主旨,同时和首段②进行呼应。这样使得整篇文章结构严谨而清晰。

2. 引用名言:通过引用一句名言或格言来支撑主旨,可以增添作文的可信度和深度。

写作实践[①]

现如今,每所学校都要求学生穿校服。请你谈谈要求穿校服这一做法的利弊。

Nowadays, almost all the students are required to wear school uniforms at school.

...

As the saying goes, each coin has two sides. Therefore, wearing school uniforms has both advantages and disadvantages. Im my opinion, we should not be lost in the argument only. What we should do is make school uniforms

① "写作实践"部分的作文题目改编自詹玲:《高考英语写作专项训练》,上海教育出版社,2010,第 10 页。

more endearing and therefore more acceptable.

点评

在这篇利弊作文的尾段中，作者通过一句格言——“each coin has two sides”（事物总有两面性）——来总结事物总有利有弊，解决问题的关键在于我们应如何让校服变得更讨人喜欢和接受度更高。

3. 提出建议或展望：根据主题，提出一些相关建议或解决方案，指明未来的发展方向或表达对未来的展望。

写作实践

Building a Better Future

…

① In conclusion, it is high time that we took immediate action to address the challenges we face. ② It is crucial that governments, organizations, and individuals prioritize sustainable practices and conservation efforts. ③ By embracing renewable energy, reducing waste, and preserving natural resources, we can create a better future for ourselves and future generations. ④ Though the road ahead may be challenging, I am confident that with determination and collective efforts, we can overcome these obstacles and create a healthier and more sustainable world.

点评

本段为全文的尾段。本文主要讲述了地球现在面临的很多挑战、问题的成因以及可以采取的措施。①②③是针对这些危机我们可以采取哪些措施；④则是作者的信念以及对未来的展望，起到了卒章显志的作用。

4. 给出启示或倡议：在尾段中，可以给读者留下一个启示或倡议，鼓励他们在日常生活中采取行动或改变自己的态度。

写作实践

随着生活条件的不断改善，越来越多的人喜欢出游度假，但遗憾的是一些游客的不文明行为屡见不鲜。请你给全校同学写一封关于文明出游的倡议书，内容须包括：

1. 你对这种现象的看法；
2. 提出倡议。

With the improvement of people's living conditions, an increasing number of people choose to go on vacation whenever possible. But it is a pity that cases where some tourists spit, litter, scribble, make loud noises, jump the queue in tourist destinations are often seen, which brings about some consequences worse than we have imagined ...

...

① Consequently, I appeal to every student to raise our civilization consciousness and be a self-disciplined tourist. When visiting resorts, we should throw rubbish into the dustbin and always keep garbage classification in mind. ② Don't make noises in public and don't spit. ③ Do wait in a line patiently and be sure not to scrawl. ④ At the same time, be sure to show our respect for local customs and tradition, and it is better not to disturb the normal life of locals.

点评

这是一封倡议书，段落中的①对学生们提出了倡议，在后面的支持句②③④中，用了 don't ...、do ... 以及 be sure to ... 几个并列结构，呼吁大家对自己的行为和态度做出改变。

当然，写好尾段的这些方法并不是单一的，可以几种方法混合使用。

此外，尾段应尽量做到简短明了、言简意赅，同时又能给读者留下深刻的印象。

四、如何写好主旨句

主旨句(thesis statement/main idea)是英语作文中至关重要的一部分，它能清晰地概括整篇文章的主题和中心思想。下面介绍一些写好主旨句的关键技巧。

(一) 明确主题

首先，需要明确文章的主题是什么，整篇文章都要围绕这一主题展开。主旨句必须直接与主题相关并清晰明了。

(二) 语言简明扼要

主旨句应该简明扼要地表达出整篇文章的中心思想，并吸引读者的注意力。不少学生为了凸显其英语水平，在主旨句中用了过于复杂的语言，反而使得主旨不清，句子生涩难懂，结果适得其反。

(三) 避免泛泛而谈

主旨句应该具体而有针对性，避免使用笼统的词语和描述。

写作实践

2002 年上海高考作文

简要描述图片内容，结合生活实际，就图片的主题谈谈自己的感想。

你们让我自己骑好吗？

学生习作：

As is vividly shown in the picture, a young girl is riding a bike, with almost all her family members around, in case anything unexpected should happen.

【简要描述图片内容】

It's a common phenomenon that parents care too much about their children. From my perspective, it's not sensible for parents to overprotect their children.【主旨句】My reasons are listed as follows.

...

点评

这是2002年的上海高考作文，要求学生简要描述图片内容并谈谈自己的感想，属于典型的夹叙夹议类文章。该学生在简要描述图片内容后，陈述了主旨句："From my perspective, it's not sensible for parents to overprotect their children."。作为主旨句，它有以下几个特征：

1. 主题明确：这句话的主题就是"过度保护孩子"。

2. 句型较简单：用了一个it结构做形式主语。

3. 语言具体，并非泛泛而谈。这位学生原来的主旨句是这样的："It is not good to overprotect their children."。"good"过于笼统，它可以指人也可指事物，所以可以用sensible替换good，并在句中加上for parents，这样主旨就更为明确清晰了。

通过合理运用这些要点，学生就可以写出一个有效的主旨句了，从而为这篇英语作文奠定良好的基础，确保整篇文章围绕着这个主旨句展开，以保证文章的逻辑性、一致性和连贯性。

五、如何写好段落

写好段落是英语写作中非常重要的一环。一个好的段落可以用图4来表示。下面从几个方面详细阐述如何写好段落。

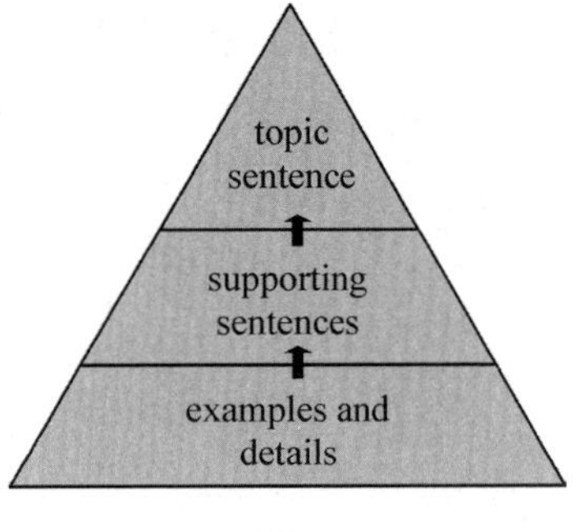

图4

(一) 主题句(topic sentence)

一个好的段落应该以一个明确、简洁的主题句开始。主题句通常位于段落的开头，它提供了段落的中心思想。

首先，一个好的主题句应使用简明扼要的语言，避免复杂的词汇和冗长的句子。很多学生为了凸显其英语水平，在写段落的主题句时用了复杂的词汇和句子，这可能使得句子的表达含义不清，重点不够突出，读者不能很快地领会这一段的主旨，效果适得其反。因此，主题句一定要做到语言简明扼要，直达要点。

其次，主题句应只包含一个要点，即"一个主题＋一个中心思想(one topic＋one controlling idea)"，过多的要点会使展开的下文层次不清，逻辑混乱。

写作实践

找出以下主题句存在的问题：

(1) Books can be a powerful tool to help me command English rules.

(2) Grammar books can help me deal with grammatical problems and improve my academic performance.

作为主题句，例(1)主题指向不清。由 Books 和 command English rules 两处可以看出，此处的 Books 应改为 Grammar books。

主题句应该遵从"one topic＋one controlling idea"的原则。在例(2)中，很明显有两个观点，故可删除"and improve my academic performance"。

(二) 支持句(supporting sentences)

支持句是主题句的补充，它们展开、解释和支撑主题句的观点。支持句应该清晰、连贯，并与主题句有逻辑上的联系。

(三) 例子和细节(examples and details)

为了使段落更具说服力和可读性，需要提供具体的例子和细节来支撑观点。例子可以是真实的或虚构的，细节应是有力的、具体的，用来阐明观点或支撑论证。

(四) 逻辑连接(logical connections)

一个好的段落应该有逻辑上的连接，从而使读者能够理解并跟随文章的思路进行阅读。可以使用过渡词或短语来引导读者进入下一个观点或支持句。一些常用的过渡词(transitional words)包括：

表并列关系：First，Second，Third；Firstly，Secondly，Thirdly；In addition；Furthermore；...

表递进关系：To plus；What makes the matter worse；More importantly；Most importantly；...

表转折关系：However；Though；Still；Nevertheless；...

表因果关系：Therefore；Consequently；As a result；...

(五) 结束句(concluding sentence)

段落的结束句应该总结或概括整个段落的主要观点。它可以对主题句进行重述，也可以向读者提出问题并引发其思考。结束句应该简洁明了，给读者一个完整的段落已经结束的信号。当然，在很多段落中，没有结束句也未尝不可。

写作实践

① Exercise plays a crucial role in maintaining a healthy lifestyle. ② Regular physical activity has numerous benefits for both our physical and mental well-being. ③ Engaging in regular exercise helps improve cardiovascular health，increase muscle strength and flexibility，and promote weight management. ④ It also reduces the risk of chronic diseases such as diabetes，heart disease，and certain types of cancer. ⑤ In addition，exercise plays a vital role in combating stress，anxiety，and depression，as it promotes the release of endorphins，the "feel-good" hormones. ⑥ In conclusion，engaging in regular exercise not only enhances our physical health but also improves our mental well-being，making it an essential component of a healthy lifestyle.

点评

这是一个非常典型的段落。①是本段的主题句，②是支持句，③④⑤从身体和精神两方面提供了很多例子和细节，⑥则是整段的总结。

整个段落为总—分—总结构，层次清晰，内容充实；通过使用 also、in addition、in conclusion 等逻辑连接词使得文章的逻辑性、连贯性、结构性较强。

总之，写好一个段落需要有明确的主题句、有效的支持句、具体的例子和细节、有逻辑连接的过渡词、恰当的结束句。相信通过反复的写作练习，学生会逐渐掌握这些技巧，写出高质量的英语作文段落。

六、如何使全文连贯通顺

在英语写作中，处理好整篇文章的逻辑关系非常重要，这可使文章更连贯通顺，让读者能够清晰地理解文章的观点和思想。下面几个方法可以帮助实现这一目标。

（一）提前构建好文章结构

在开始写作前，先构思文章的整体框架和主要内容。确定好文章的开头、中间和结尾，并列出要点，以便在写作过程中有一个明确的方向。这个过程就是我们在前面谈到的——“如何谋篇布局”。

（二）使用合适的连接词和过渡词

连接词和过渡词是连接句子和段落的纽带。例如，使用 however 表示转折、in addition 表示增加信息、therefore 表示因果关系等。合理运用这些词汇可以将不同的思想和段落连接起来，使文章变得流畅。

（三）维持好段内句子之间的逻辑性和一致性

段落中的句子是围绕着本段的主题句展开的，保持段落中句子之间的一致性、连贯性，可以增强文章的逻辑性，同时确保每个句子都与主题有关。

（四）维持好段落之间的逻辑性和一致性

段落之间也应该有明确的主题和逻辑关系。如果段落之间是并列关系，就可用 first、second、third 等来表明其逻辑关系；如果段落之间为因果关系，就可用 therefore、as a result 等连接词表明其逻辑关系；等等。

学生通过运用这些方法，就能处理好整篇英语作文各个段落之间的逻辑关系，使文章的观点清晰明了、语言连贯通顺。

第二节　写 作 技 巧

在了解了写作过程后，我们还需要掌握一些写作技巧，这样能使得文章更加有理有据、真实可信。英语作文的写作技巧有很多种，下面详细阐述一些常用的写作技巧。

一、对比法

对比法(Comparison and Contrast)是通过对比两个或多个事物之间的相似点和不同点，来阐述作者对某一问题的观点。对比法可以用来解释原因、分析影响、陈述优势等。对比法是上海高考英语写作中常用的技巧。

以下是使用对比法写作的案例：

作品一：《过雪天》

Snowflakes falling gently to the ground,
Children building snowmen of delight,
Laughter filling the crisp and frosty air.

作品二：《夏日风景》

Strolling through a summer paradise,
Sunshine casting its warm and golden rays,
Fragrant flowers blooming in vibrant hues,
Joyful voices echoing through the balmy breeze.

这两首诗歌使用对比法来描述冬天和夏天的不同景象和感受。通过对比使用的词语，表现的情感和气息等的差异，读者可以清晰地感受到两个季节的不同魅力。在作品一中，诗人描述在冬天漫步的场景：雪花轻柔地落在地上，孩子们兴高采烈地堆雪人，清爽而寒冷的空气里充盈着欢声笑语。这种描述传达出冬天的静谧与欢乐。作品二描绘了夏季的景象：人们在夏天的乐园漫步，阳光散发着温暖的、金色的光芒，香气四溢的花朵以充满活力的色彩盛开，快乐的声音在温暖的微风中回荡。这种描绘呈现出夏天阳光明媚、花香四溢以及轻松愉快的特点。通过对比冬天和夏天的不同特征，给读者带来了截然不同的感受和视觉体验。这个例子展示了如何利用对比法来突出两个不同事物之间的差异，以此激发读者的情感和想象力。

为了使得文章更为通顺和富有逻辑性，我们在使用对比法时，可以用到以下连接词或词组：

1. however/nevertheless（然而）：用于引出对比的另一种观点或情况。

e.g. The weather forecast predicted a sunny day; however, it ended up raining heavily.

天气预报说今天是晴天，然而最后下起了大雨。

2. ..., while ...（然而）：用于表示前后两种情况的不同之处。

e.g. As we all know, people in the south of China like rice, while those in the north like cooked wheaten food.

众所周知，南方人喜欢吃大米，而北方人喜欢吃面食。

3. On the one hand ... On the other hand ...（一方面……另一方面）：用于引出两种相对立的观点或情况。

e.g. On the one hand, technology has made communication easier and faster. On the other hand, it has also led to a decrease in face-to-face interaction.

一方面，技术使交流更容易、更快捷；另一方面，它也导致了面对面交流的减少。

4. in/by contrast 或 in comparison（相比之下）：用于表示对比的两个事物之间的差异。

e. g. The city has a vibrant nightlife, while the countryside, in/by contrast, offers tranquility and fresh air.

城市有充满活力的夜生活，而乡村相反，提供宁静和新鲜的空气。

e.g. All of our other activities would pale in comparison with sky diving.

与跳伞相比，我们其他的所有活动都逊色多了。

5. on the contrary（恰恰相反）：用于表示与前面提到的观点或情况相反的情况。

e. g. Many people believe that money brings happiness, but on the contrary, some of the richest individuals are often the most unhappy.

许多人相信金钱能带来幸福，但恰恰相反，一些最富有的人往往是最不快乐的。

写作实践

浦东新区 2023 届高三二模作文

假期即将来临，你的朋友李华计划完成一篇调查报告，他对是去公共图书馆还是去自习室(self-study room)写报告犹豫不决，现征求你的建议。请参考以下信息，写一封邮件，内容须包括：

1. 你的建议；
2. 你建议的理由。(使用对比法)

	公共图书馆	自习室
收费标准	免费	20 元/5 小时
开放时间	9:00 a.m.-5:00 p.m.	24 小时
交通时长	45 分钟	10 分钟
设施环境	免费使用馆内资源	免费茶点

作为书信的首段，第一句是好朋友之间的寒暄，第二句交代了写信的事由，第三句为写信的意图并明确表明了自己的观点。首段结构清晰，内容完整。

Dear Li Hua,

I feel so happy to hear from you. I understand that you're having difficulty deciding whether to go to the public library or the self-study room to complete your survey report. After considering the information provided, I would recommend you to go to the public library.

第二段的首句为主题句。段中通过使用 on the other hand 表明了转折关系，此处使用了对比法的写作技巧。

Firstly, the public library offers free access to its resources, which can greatly benefit your research.【主题句】They have a wide range of books, magazines, and online databases that you can utilize to gather information and make your report more comprehensive. On the other hand, the self-study room may not have as many resources available.

第三段和第四段的首句都为主题句。这两段也同样用了对比法的写作技巧。

Secondly, the library indeed offers a conducive environment for studying.【主题句】Although there may be people walking around, the overall atmosphere remains quiet and conducive to concentration. The comfortable seating and minimal distractions allow you to focus on your work effectively. In comparison, the self-study room might provide a peaceful setting, but it may not match the library's level of tranquility due to the presence of other individuals working or studying.

Lastly, in terms of the opening time, I prefer the public library.【主题句】The public library is open from 9:00 a.m. to 5:00 p.m. That gives you plenty of time to work in a quiet and focused environment. While the self-study room is open around the clock, I don't think it is a necessity for you.

Considering the free resources, quiet environment, and appropriate opening hours, I reckon the public library is the ideal place for you to write your report.

总结了信件前面提到的三个方面，再次重申公共图书馆是个理想的写报告的地方。用到了总结和重申主题的尾段写作方法。

Good luck, and I hope your report turns out great!

最后祝自己的好朋友能够好运，写出好的报告，充分体现了读者意识。

Best regards,

Li Ming

二、因果分析法

因果分析法(Cause and Effect)是通过分析事件或行为之间的因果关系，以揭示某一行动的结果或原因。这种写作方法常用于解释现象、分析问题和提出建议。

1. 因果分析法可以用来展开整篇文章。

写作实践

The Effects of Smoking on Health

① Smoking is a widespread habit around the world; however, it has numerous detrimental effects on an individual's health.【主旨句】

② What makes smoking so widespread?【主题句】One of the primary causes of smoking is peer pressure. Many individuals, especially adolescents, start smoking to fit in with their social group. Furthermore, stress and anxiety are also common triggers for smoking. People often turn to cigarettes as a way to cope with their emotions or relieve tension. Lastly, the addictive nature of nicotine can also be considered a cause of smoking. Once addicted, smokers find it challenging to quit.【起因】

③ Smoking can lead to various health problems.【主题句】Firstly, it significantly increases the risk of developing lung cancer. The harmful chemicals in tobacco smoke damage the lung tissues, resulting in the formation of cancerous cells. Secondly, smoking damages the cardiovascular system, leading to an increased risk of heart disease, stroke, and high blood pressure. Thirdly, it weakens the immune system, making smokers more susceptible to infections and diseases. Lastly, it has adverse effects on oral health, causing tooth decay, gum disease, and bad breath.【结果 1】

④ Not only does smoking harm physical health, but it also has detrimental effects on mental well-being.【主题句】Nicotine acts as a stimulant, temporarily improving mood and concentration. However, prolonged use can lead to dependency, anxiety, and depression. Additionally, smoking often negatively impacts social relationships. The smell of smoke can be off-putting to non-smokers, leading to social isolation and strained personal connections.【结果 2】

⑤ In conclusion, smoking is a habit with numerous causes and significant effects on health. It is crucial for individuals, especially young people, to be aware of these harmful consequences. By understanding the causes and effects of smoking, we can make informed decisions to prioritize our well-being and work towards a tobacco-free society.【总结】

点评

这是一篇典型的现象类说明文，结构为：

段①　引入现象并指出吸烟有害健康(phenomenon/problem)

段②　吸烟的起因(causes 1&2&3)

段③④　吸烟的结果(effects 1&2)

段⑤　总结(conclusion)

整篇文章运用了因果分析法，通过分析吸烟的起因和结果，清楚地对该现象进行了阐述。

2. 因果分析法也可以用来展开一个段落。

写作实践

2023—2024 学年　上海市川沙中学 11 月校测作文

假如你是明启中学的高三学生李华，发现班级同学们在活动课上不积极参加体育活动课：有的同学回到教室看书自习，有的同学坐在操场边聊天。请给学校相关负责人写一封邮件，内容须包括：

1. 简述活动课现状；

2. 对如何改变这一现象提出建议，并给出理由。

以引入观察到的现象开始本段，建议学校应向学生强调体育锻炼的重要性。

To someone who may concern,

I hope this letter finds you well. As a senior student of our school, I am writing to shed light on a serious problem. I recently noticed that my classmates don't actively take part in exercise during PE lessons, with some reading books, doing assignments and others sitting beside the playground, chatting. In terms of this phenomenon, I'd like to share several humble opinions of my own.

① To begin with, our school may as well emphasize the significance of physical exercise to students.【主题句】② Many students skip PE lessons out of their personal prejudice, considering PE lessons trivial or unimportant while overly prioritizing studies, without coming to realize the physical well-being is fundamental to all achievements. ③ It is due to the huge amounts of academic pressure that we students need to do sufficient exercise to relax and strengthen our bodies. ④ Teachers should tell students more about this perspective so as to make them willing to exercise for themselves instead of being pushed.

②③句为原因分析，④为结果。整个段落使用了因果分析法的写作技巧。

Apart from that, more variety of physical activities should be added. There are also students who find the activities they are interested in, thus skipping the class. Consequently, teachers may consider adding some special activities such as Tai Chi, or other novel and interesting ones that appeal to teenagers. This would greatly motivate them as well.

In conclusion, the situation can be improved by laying more emphasis on physical exercise and adding new sorts of physical activities. I sincerely hope that you can consider my suggestion.

Yours sincerely,

Li Hua

可见,不管是写作整篇文章还是个别段落,我们都可以使用因果分析法。

为了使得文章更为通顺和有逻辑性,我们在使用因果分析法时,可以用到以下几组关系词:

起因(cause):because, since, as a result of, because of, due to, ...

结果(effect):therefore, consequently, thus, hence, ...

三、列举法

列举法(Enumeration)是通过逐个列举事物,详细介绍各个事物之间的关系。这种方法常用于描述一个主题下的各个方面、具体细节等。

以下是一个列举法的案例:

My Favourite Activities

My life is full of colourful activities. They can bring me joy, help me relax, and contribute positively to my overall well-being.

1. Reading

Reading is one of my favourite activities as it allows me to explore new worlds, gain knowledge, and expand my imagination. Whether it's fictional novels, self-help books, or informative articles, reading enables me to relax and escape from the pressures of daily life. It also enhances my vocabulary and improves my writing skills.

2. Painting

Painting is another activity that brings me immense joy. It provides a creative outlet for self-expression and allows me to convey my emotions and thoughts onto the canvas. Using various colours, shades, and techniques, I can create beautiful artwork that reflects my inner self. Painting also helps me relax and reduces stress, acting as a form of therapy for me.

3. Playing the guitar

Playing the guitar is not only a hobby but also a way for me to unwind. It allows me to express myself musically and connect with others through music. Strumming the strings and creating melodies is a fantastic way to relax and alleviate any tensions or worries. Moreover, playing the guitar challenges me to improve my skills and learn new songs, which brings a sense of accomplishment.

...

In conclusion, reading, painting, playing the guitar, exercising, and cooking are my favourite activities. These activities provide me with relaxation, self-expression, enjoyment, and personal growth. Engaging in these activities enables me to find joy and balance in life, contributing positively to my overall well-being.

点评

本文通过阿拉伯数字1、2、3等列举了自己喜欢的活动。当然，在写作列举时，也可以用到以下几组连接词：

1. Firstly, Secondly, Thirdly, Finally; ...

2. In addition, Furthermore, Moreover, Besides,...

3. At first, Next, Then, At last; ...

四、举例法

举例法(Example)是通过举例子来支撑自己的观点或论证。举例法可以使文章更加具体而生动,更具说服力和可信度。

写作实践

2022 年 *Shanghai Students' Post* 高考专刊 12 月

假设你是明启中学的学生李平,学校英语报正在举办主题为“The Current Trend and My life”的征文活动。请写一篇文章投稿,介绍你身边的流行趋势,主要内容包括:

1. 简述所选趋势的背景情况;
2. 该趋势对你生活的影响。

Artificial Intelligence — One of the Most Popular Trends in Technology Today

Artificial Intelligence (AI) is one of today's hottest trends. Its popularity can be seen in all walks of modern life. In recent years we have seen many AI-based applications spring up like mushrooms, such as those connected with robots, mobile payment methods and so forth. Its increasing importance can also be seen in education, where AI courses being offered at many universities are increasingly attracting students. In my own personal life, AI has helped to put my life on the right track.

First of all, with the help of AI, I am able to enjoy a better quality of life. 【主题句】For instance, once I am finished with my school day and have arrived home exhausted, the last thing I have to think about is making myself something to eat. This is where my smart rice cooker comes in handy. It can prepare delightful snacks and relieve me of the pressure to have to cook for myself, which allows me to both conserve and refresh my energy. 【例 1】

What's more, AI makes my life much more convenient.【主题句】In the office building where my father works, I once encountered some robots that were delivering parcels and takeaway food in an orderly and efficient manner. That day, I ordered myself a cup of milk tea and my beverage was delivered to me in an instant. Everything about the delivery process was automated.【例 2】

Last but not least, AI helps to support my life with its collection of "big data".【主题句】For example, my AI doctor can tailor whatever treatments I may need to my previous medical records, which results in my receiving better medical service. This means that I can recover faster with less pain.【例 3】

I firmly believe that the craze for AI services is something that will eventually sweep across the entire world. If we can take advantage of it wisely, we will all be able to enjoy a brighter future.

点评

这篇文章从 AI 的趋势入手,先简要描述了这个趋势,然后从 AI 能够让"我"享受高品质的生活、能够让"我"的生活更为便捷以及能够用大数据帮助"我"的生活三个方面进行阐述,并在每个方面举了一个实例进行说明,使得文章生动翔实,更具有说服力。

在写作时,可以用到以下几组连接词:

1. such as/like 例如,好像

e.g. I enjoy outdoor activities, such as/like hiking, swimming, and camping.

我喜欢户外活动,比如远足、游泳和露营。

2. for example/for instance 例如

e.g. For instance, in a business setting, there are various departments such as marketing, finance, human resources, operations, and sales.

例如,在商业环境中,有不同的部门,如市场营销、财务、人力资源、运营和销售。

3. take ... as an example 以……为例

e.g. Take Mary, my best friend, as an example.

以我最好的朋友玛丽为例。

五、定义法

定义法(Definition)是通过分析某一概念的定义，来详细说明它的含义和特点。定义法可以用于阐述某个概念的重要性、划定范围等。

谚语、格言类作文的首段就需对该谚语或格言进行定义和解释。

写作实践

2005 年上海高考作文

古人云："天生我材必有用。(There must be a use for my talent.)"通过描述你生活中的一件事，说明人各有所长，无论才能大小，都能成为有用的人。

(首段) As the old saying goes, "There must be a use for my talent." From my perspective, the essence of this saying lies in that each individual is born with unique talents. By recognizing and fully utilizing our talents, we can contribute to society in our own unique way.

点评

这是这篇文章的首段，首先引出此谚语，然后揭示其重要性，最后对此谚语进行解释和定义。

六、描述法

描述法(Description)是通过详细的描述，使读者对事物有更加直观的了解。描述法常用于写景、描写人物，以及描述图片、图表等。

(一) 图表类

图表类文章的首段需要对图表进行简要描述。

写作实践

学校在“读书节”的时候，就学生阅读经典名著的情况进行了一次调查。以下是你班的调查数据，请就此写一份报告给学校，并简单谈谈你的想法。

学生总数	每天阅读	经常阅读	偶尔阅读	从不阅读
46	0	2	8	36

Recently, a survey has been carried out on how often students read classics. As can be seen from the table, nearly eighty percent of the participants never read. Some read occasionally and few read very often. Unfortunately, nobody keeps reading every day.

点评

图表类作文的首段需要描述图表所显示的内容，引出需要描述的核心部分，揭示主旨。注意，数据的引用不需要面面俱到。

（二）图片类

图片类文章的首段同样需要对图片进行简要描述。

写作实践

2010 年上海高考作文

右图是小学新生的课堂一角，对照你当时的上课情况，做出比较并谈谈你的感受。你的作文必须包括：

1. 描述图片里学生上课的场景；
2. 比较你同时期的上课情况；
3. 简单谈谈你的感受。

① In a classroom of a primary school sit several children, who are new to the school. They put up their hands and hold their heads up high, expecting to be called by the teacher. You can tell their excitement through the happy look on their faces. So that's what the picture all about.

② This picture takes me back to when I was in primary school. At that moment, I, as well as all the other kids had to follow the strict school rules. We sat in class quietly, listening to the teacher without saying much. There were not many live discussions among us. Not only were we scared to answer the teacher's questions, but also we never dared to ask the teacher any ourselves because we were afraid of getting it wrong.

…

点评

这是2010年的高考作文题。段①先对该图片进行了描述，段②则是对同时期作者自己的上课情况进行描述。通过两者的对比，谈了自己的感想。这篇高考作文要求学生将对比法和描述法相结合。

七、记叙法

记叙法(Narration)是通过讲述一个故事或个人经历来支撑观点或强调主题。记叙法可以使文章更加生动有趣，吸引读者的注意力。

写作实践[①]

根据生活实例，谈谈对“There is no shortcut to success.(成功无捷径)”这句话的理解。

① “写作实践”部分的作文题目及范文来自詹玲：《高考英语写作专项训练》，上海教育出版社，2010，第94页，第139—140页。作文题目及范文均有做改动。

When I was young, I often asked Mum whether there was a shortcut to writing a good composition or achieving high in my maths test. My mother always looked me in the eye, smiling, "My dear, there is no shortcut to success." At first, I did not believe her. However, as time goes by, I come to realize the true meaning of this saying. Many instances in my life have told me that success can only be achieved with perseverance and great efforts. If one is too eager for instant success or benefit, the result might be the opposite to what he wishes for.

这是一篇格言类文章，首段运用了定义法。

Take my experience in learning the guitar as an example. Years ago, I decided to learn to play the guitar. I was eager to master the instrument quickly and impress my friends. So, I bought a guitar and a few books on guitar techniques, hoping to pick up the skill in a matter of weeks.

However, as I progressed, I realized that there was no quick fix. I had to spend hours practicing, learning the scales, and memorizing the chords. My fingers were sore, and progress was slow. At times, I felt discouraged and considered giving up.

第二至第四段运用了记叙法，通过讲述自己学吉他的一个事例来说明"成功无捷径"。

But I persisted. I kept practicing, day after day, week after week. Gradually, I began to see improvements. My playing became smoother, and I started to enjoy the process of learning. Eventually, I was able to play some simple songs and even impress a few of my friends.

Looking back, I realize that if I had tried to take a shortcut and skipped the hard work, I would never have achieved my goal. It was the dedication and efforts that led to my success.

As the saying goes, "The longest way around is the nearest way home." This is the policy we should follow in pursuit of success.

尾段通过使用一句格言来总结全文。

八、分类法

分类法(Classification)是根据事物或人的种类或属性进行分类，并对每一个类别进行详细描述和分析。这种写作方法有助于为此类事物或人提供全面完整的信息。

写作实践

2018年上海秋考作文

假设你是明启中学高三学生卢平，校英文报向高三学生征文，题目是"My Teachers"，卢平也想投稿。具体要求是：

1. 请你将认识的老师进行分类；
2. 具体描述每一类老师的特征。

My Teachers

As a senior student at Mingqi High School, I have encountered various types of teachers throughout my academic journey. When it comes

to categorizing them, there are three distinct groups that come to mind. 【主旨句】

Firstly, there are knowledgeable teachers. 【主题句】 These teachers possess a deep understanding of their subject matter and are able to explain complex concepts with ease. They stimulate our curiosity and inspire us to delve deeper into the subjects they teach. They make learning enjoyable and instill in us a passion for the subject.

Secondly, we have caring teachers. 【主题句】 These teachers not only focus on our academic development but also pay attention to our personal well-being. They are understanding and empathetic, always ready to lend a listening ear and provide guidance. They create a warm and nurturing environment that makes us feel comfortable and supported.

Lastly, we have strict teachers. 【主题句】 Although their teaching style may seem intimidating at times, their high expectations push us to strive for excellence. They are strict because they care about our success and want to prepare us for future challenges. Though demanding, they teach us valuable lessons in discipline and resilience.

In conclusion, my teachers can be categorized into knowledgeable, caring, and strict groups. 【概括总结】 Each group contributes to my personal growth in different ways, helping me to become a well-rounded individual. I am grateful to have such dedicated educators in my school. 【表示感谢】

点评

这是一篇高考真题。作者把老师分为知识渊博型、关爱型和严格型三类，并对每一种类型进行了具体的描述。最后的总结部分先对上文的三种类型进行概括，而后对老师表达了自己的感谢。整篇文章结构非常清晰，逻辑连贯，运用了分类法和描述法相结合的写作技巧。

综上所述，根据题目的要求，结合具体情况，选用一种或多种写作技巧，能够帮助我们充分、清晰、流畅地表达出我们的观点和思想。

第三节　写 作 语 言

学生在学习并熟练掌握英语写作过程和写作技巧后，接下来就要学习如何使写作语言具有多样性和丰富性。写作语言的多样性表现为使用不同的词汇、短语和句型等来表达相同的意思，丰富性表现为运用各种语法结构、时态和语态来构建复杂的句子。学生通过学习具有多样性和丰富性的写作语言，不仅能提升文章的可读性，展现其词汇储备量和语言表达能力，还能进一步培养和发展英语学科核心素养。

一、写作语言的注意事项

以下是高中英语写作中语言处理方面的一些常见注意事项：

1. 语法：良好的语法是英语写作的基础。务必正确使用时态、语态、动词形式和句子结构等，并注意主谓一致和时态一致。

2. 拼写和标点：正确的拼写和标点对于准确传达信息非常重要。要反复检查并纠正拼写错误，使用适当的标点符号来分隔和组织句子。

3. 词汇使用：选择恰当的词汇来表达自己的意思，使文章更具有准确性和丰富性。注重平时的词汇积累，避免重复使用相同的词汇，学会使用同义词等。

4. 句子结构和语言：使用多种句式和恰当的连词或过渡词，使文章更加丰富、流畅和连贯，内容更易于理解。避免使用冗长或啰唆的句子，删除不必要的修饰语或重复的信息，运用简洁明了的表达方式，使句子简洁有力。

5. 框架结构：有意识地组织和安排写作结构，以确保文章的逻辑性和条理性。使用段落来划分不同的主题，学会使用主题句。

6. 语言风格：发展并形成自己的语言风格，使写作更具个性和吸引力，但同时也要避免使用过于复杂或模糊的表达方式。

二、亮点词汇

100组高分亮点词汇 vs 普通词汇

意　　义	高分亮点词汇	普通词汇
认为，主张	argue/maintain/hold	think
赢得，取得	earn/gain/reap	win
重要的，决定性的	vital/crucial/critical/decisive	important
考虑	take sth. into consideration/reflect on/meditate on/ponder over	consider
下结论	draw the conclusion/arrive at the conclusion/come into conclusion	in a word
支持，赞成	approve of/in favor of/stand by one's side	agree with
利用	make best use of/make full use of	use
描绘，描述	depict/picture	describe
当前，目前	at present/currently/presently	now
聪明的，有才智的	intelligent/bright/brilliant	clever
疲惫的	exhausted/fatigued/worn-out/weary	tired
阻碍，阻止	hinder/hamper	stop
好处，优点	advantage/merit	strong point
坏处，缺点	disadvantage/defect/flaw/drawback/deficiency	weak point
集中精神于	concentrate on/center on	focus on
参加	participate in/engage in	join
记住	bear in mind/keep in mind	remember
依赖，依靠	rely on/lean on	depend on
珍惜	cherish	value

续　表

意　　义	高分亮点词汇	普通词汇
破坏	devastate	destroy
遇到	come across/encounter	meet
解释	account for/illustrate/clarify	explain
沮丧的，失意的	frustrated/discouraged/depressed	sad
致力于，尽力做	commit oneself to	try one's best
渴望	yearn/thirst/long for	be eager for
发展	advancement	development
成就	achievement/accomplishment/fulfillment	success
流行的	prevalent/fashionable	popular
目击	witness	see/watch
除……之外	apart from/in addition to/along with	besides
出现	emerge/arise	appear
快速增加	rocket/multiply	increase rapidly
消失	vanish，fade away	disappear
恶化	deteriorate	worsen
面临	be confronted with	face
评价	evaluate	judge
执行	implement	carry out
显然的	apparent	obvious
好的，优秀的	outstanding/remarkable/distinguished/excellent	good
实现	accomplish/fulfill/achieve	realize
迷人的，吸引人的	charming/appealing/fascinating/attractive	pretty/beautiful
令人兴奋的	thrilling	exciting

续　表

意　　义	高分亮点词汇	普通词汇
喜悦的	overjoyed	glad/happy
显示	reveal/indicate/demonstrate	show
通知	notify/inform	tell
培养	cultivate/develop	train
说服	convince	persuade
为了	for the sake of/on the purpose of	in order to
事实上	in reality/in effect/as a matter of fact	in fact
给予，捐赠	contribute/denote	give
方法，手段	method/approach/means/measure	way
唯一的，仅有的	sole/single/unique	only
教导	tutor/coach/educate	teach
倾向于，往往	be inclined to/tend to/be liable to	always
充足的	abundant/sufficient	enough
最终	ultimately/eventually	finally
在我看来	for my part/from my perspective	in my opinion
想出，想到	come up with/occur to sb.	think
与……相联系	be connected with/be linked to/be relevant to	be related to
需要	call for/require/demand	need
建设性的，有益的	constructive/beneficial/rewarding	useful
熟悉，知道	be acquainted with/be familiar with/be informed of	know
必要的，不可缺少的	indispensable/essential	necessary
意识到	be aware of/be conscious of	realize

续　表

意　义	高分亮点词汇	普通词汇
决心做	be determined to do/make up one's mind to do	decide to do
明白,理解	comprehend	understand
因为	due to/owing to/thanks to/result from	because
巨大的	tremendous/immense/gigantic/enormous	big/large
很多的	countless/numberless/numerous	many
非常,十分	extremely/exceedingly	very
数字	figure/statistic	number
上升	mount/roar	increase/rise
引发	trigger/arouse	cause
忍受	endure/put up with	bear
询问	inquire	ask
能力	capability/competence/capacity/faculty	ability
壮丽的	splendid/magnificent/impressive/marvelous	grand
繁荣的,富裕的	prosperous/flourishing/thriving/booming	rich
各种各样的	a variety of/various/diverse	all kinds of
保存	conserve	save/keep
古老的	ancient	old
享有	enjoy/possess	have
违反,侵犯	violate/disobey/infringe	break
由……组成	consist of/be composed of/be comprised of	be made up of
一些	a slice of/quiet a few	some
事情	affair/business/matter	thing
普通的	shared	common

续 表

意 义	高分亮点词汇	普通词汇
越来越	increasing(ly)/growing	more and more
某人感兴趣……	sth. appeals to sb./sth. exerts a tremendous fascination on sb.	sb. be interested in
反对	frown on	be against/disagree with
举例	to name just a few	for example
一般而言	by and large	in general
以……为理由	on the ground of	because of
根据	in accordance with	according to
不惜任何代价	by all means	at all costs
来自,源于	stem from/derive from	come from
表达	voice/convey	express
全面地	thoroughly	completely
解决,处理	cope with/resolve	deal with
优于	superior to	better than

三、常用谚语与习语

Achieve twice the result with half the effort.	事半功倍。
Actions speak louder than words.	行胜于言。
A friend in need is a friend indeed.	患难见真情。
All roads lead to Rome.	条条大路通罗马。
All that glitters is not gold.	不是所有发光的都是金子。

All work and no play makes Jack a dull boy.	只工作不玩耍，聪明的孩子也变傻。
As you sow, so will you reap.	种瓜得瓜，种豆得豆。
A timely snow promises a good harvest.	瑞雪兆丰年。
Diligence can make up for lack of intelligence.	勤能补拙。
Don't judge a book by its cover.	不要以貌取人。
Don't put off till tomorrow what should be done today.	今日事，今日毕。
Early to bed and early to rise makes a man healthy, wealthy and wise.	早睡早起身体好。
Each coin has two sides.	事物总有两面性。
Every minute counts.	分秒必争。
Failure is the mother of success.	失败乃成功之母。
Genius is one percent inspiration and ninety-nine percent perspiration.	天才是 1%的灵感加 99%的汗水。
Health is better than wealth.	健康胜过财富。
He who has never been to the Great Wall is not a true man.	不到长城非好汉。
He who laughs last laughs best.	谁笑到最后，谁笑得最好。
He who plays with fire gets burned.	玩火者必自焚。
Honesty is the best policy.	诚实不欺为上策。
Hope for the best, and prepare for the worst.	抱最好的希望，做最坏的打算。
It's never too late to learn.	活到老，学到老。
It's never too late to mend.	亡羊补牢，未为迟也。

It is no use crying over spilt milk.	覆水难收。
Knowledge is power.	知识就是力量。
Like father, like son.	有其父必有其子。
Look before you leap./Think twice before you do.	三思而后行。
Lost time is never found again.	岁月既往,一去不回。
Money is the root of all evil.	金钱是万恶之源。
More haste, less speed.	欲速则不达。
No pains, no gains./No gains without pains.	不劳则无获。
Out of sight, out of mind.	眼不见,心不念(烦)。
Practice makes perfect.	熟能生巧。
Prevention is better than cure.	预防胜于治疗。
Pride goes before a fall./Pride will have a fall.	骄傲使人落后/骄者必败。
Rome was not built in a day.	伟业非一日之功/冰冻三尺非一日之寒。
Seeing is believing.	眼见为实。
Strike while the iron is hot.	趁热打铁。
The early bird catches the worm.	早起的鸟儿有虫吃。/捷足先登。
The spirit is willing, but the flesh is weak.	心有余而力不足。
There is no accounting for tastes.	人各有所好。
There is no rule but has exceptions.	有规则必有例外。
Time and tide wait for no man.	岁月不等人。
Two heads are better than one.	三个臭皮匠,顶个诸葛亮。
Unity is strength.	团结就是力量。

Vary from person to person./Depend on the individual.	因人而异。
Well begun is half done.	良好的开端是成功的一半。
Where there is a will, there is a way.	有志者事竟成。
When in Rome, do as the Romans do.	入乡随俗。

四、常用写作句型

高中英语写作不仅要求词汇丰富，富于变化，也要求句型结构具有多样性。下面是写作中常用的40个句型结构及其例句。

1. As is known (to us all) ... = It is known (to us all)+that 从句=What is known to all is+that 从句　众所周知……

例：众所周知，运动有助于健康。(3种句式)

As is known (to us all), exercise does good to health.

It is known (to us all) that exercise does good to health.

What is known to all is that exercise does good to health.

2. It is believed/thought that sb./sth. ... = sb./sth. is believed to do ... 人们普遍认为……

例：人们普遍认为人工智能是自互联网发明以来最重要的进步。(2种句式)

It is believed that Artificial Intelligence is the most important advance since the Internet was invented.

Artificial Intelligence is believed to be the most important advance since the Internet was invented.

3. It never occurred to sb.+that 从句 = It didn't occur to sb.+that 从句　某人从没想到过……

例：我从没想到过我会在机场碰到我的老朋友。(2种句式)

It never occurred to me that I would encounter my old friend at the airport.

It didn't occur to me that I would encounter my old friend at the airport.

4. It is no good/use doing ... 做……无用

例：我认为为做过的事情后悔是没有用的。

I think it no use crying over spilt milk.

5. It is likely that sb./sth. ... = sb./sth. is likely to do ... 某人/某事可能……

例：因为不良的饮食习惯，西方人比亚洲人更容易得心脏病。(2种句式)

It is more likely that Westerners will have heart disease than Asians because of bad eating habits.

Westerners are more likely to have heart disease than Asians because of bad eating habits.

6. It is hard to imagine/say/believe ... 很难想象/说/相信……

例：很难想象他在如此短的时间内已为那即将到来的面试做好了充分准备。

It is hard to imagine he has fully prepared for the coming interview in such a short time.

7. (It is) no wonder (that) ... 难怪……

例：因为他把太多的时间用在了玩电脑游戏上，难怪这次考试没通过。

(It is) no wonder (that) he failed to pass the exam because he had spent too much time playing computer games.

8. When it comes to sb./sth./doing sth. ... 当谈到……

例：当谈到如何高效地工作，每个人的观点都不一样。

When it comes to how to work efficiently, views vary from person to person.

9. It is still a question whether ... =Whether ... is still a question.

It remains a question whether ... =Whether ... remains a question. ……依然是个疑问

例：我们的运动会明天是否能按计划举行依然是个疑问。(4种句式)

It remains a question whether our sports meet will take place as planned tomorrow. =Whether our sports meet will take place as planned tomorrow remains a question.

It is still a question whether our sports meet will take place as planned tomorrow. =Whether our sports meet will take place as planned tomorrow is still a question.

10. What (really) matters (to sb.) is ...　对……而言重要的是……

例：对我们来说真正重要的不是你说什么，而是你做什么。

What (really) matters (to us) is not what you say but what you do.

11. keep/bear sb./sth. in mind = keep/bear in mind+that 从句　牢记

例：我认为每个人都应该记住这个词。

I think everybody should keep/bear this word in mind.

例：请牢记你必须晚上 11 点钟之前回家。

Keep/Bear in mind that you have to be home by 11 p.m.

12. take sth. for granted　认为……理所当然

例：我想当然地认为终有一天他会成功。(2 种句式)

I take it for granted that he will succeed one day.

It is taken for granted that he will succeed one day.

13. see to sth.　负责，照料；处理

例：你负责安排下次会议，好吗？

Will you see to the arrangements for the next meeting?

see to it that ... = make sure that ... =ensure that ...　照料好；确保……

例：请确保完成这份工作。(2 种句式)

See to it that the work is done.

Make sure that the work is done.

14. I would appreciate it (very much) if you could do sth.　如果你做……我将万分感激

例：如果你能采纳我的建议，我将万分感激。

I would appreciate it (very much) if you could adopt my advice.

15. It is up to sb. to do sth.　做某事取决于某人

例：该你做决定了。

It is up to you to make a decision.

16. 强调句型：

（1）It be＋被强调部分＋that 从句

（2）sb. do/does/did＋动词原形

例：他昨天在图书馆读了三本书。

It was in the library that he read three books yesterday.

例：我真的喜欢这个假期。

I do enjoy the vacation.

17. not ... until ... ＝It is/was not until＋被强调部分＋that 从句＝Not until ...　直到……才……

例：直到晚上 11 点钟他才回来。（3 种句式）

He didn't come back until 11 p.m.

It was not until 11 p.m. that he came back.

Not until 11 p.m. did he come back.

18. no sooner ... than ... ＝ hardly ... when ...　一……就……

例：我刚走，她就打电话来了。（2 种句式）

I had no sooner left than she called.

No sooner had I left than she called.

例：我们刚训练，就开始下雨了。（2 种句式）

We had hardly started training when it began to rain.

Hardly had we started training when it began to rain.

19. 名词/形容词/副词＋as/though＋主语＋谓语　虽然……

例：虽然他是个孩子，但是他懂得帮助别人。

Child as/though he is, he knows to help others.

例：虽然他还小，但已经能自力更生了。

Young as/though he is, he is able to live on himself.

20. 疑问词＋ever 引导的让步状语从句

引导词有 whatever、whichever、whoever、wherever、whenever 等，可转换为 no matter 和 what、which、who、where、when 等连用的形式。句型有：However/No matter how＋形容词/副词＋主语＋谓语，Whatever/No matter what＋谓语，等等。

例：不论困难有多大，我们都能克服。

However/No matter how great the difficulties are, we can overcome them.

例：无论发生什么事情，我们都要坚持下去。

Whatever/No matter what happens, we must stick to it.

21. There is no point/sense in doing ...　做……没有意义

例：提过去那些无聊的事毫无意义。

There is no point in mentioning the dull events in the past.

22. There is no need (for sb.) to do ...　没有必要做……

例：我们没必要老为这些鸡毛蒜皮的事争执。

There is no need for us to keep arguing about such trifles.

23. There is no doubt+that 从句　毫无疑问

例：毫无疑问，电话和传真是重要的通信方式。

There is no doubt that telephone and fax are important means of communication.

24. There is no possibility of =There is no possibility+that 从句　……没有可能

例：人类将不可能被机器控制。(2 种句式)

There is no possibility of humans being controlled by machines.

There is no possibility that humans will be controlled by machines.

25. (The) chances are+that 从句　很可能……

例：很可能人类将最终登陆火星。

(The) chances are that man will eventually land on Mars.

26. There is no denying+that 从句　不可否认

例：不可否认，台湾是我们祖国不可分割的一部分。

There is no denying that Taiwan is an inalienable part of our motherland.

27. Those+who 引导的定语从句　……的人

例：那些考试不及格的人寒假必须参加补考。

Those who failed the exam must take a makeup exam in the winter holiday.

28. 部分倒装：(1) Only+状语(状语从句、介词短语、副词)+助动词/情态

动词＋主语＋动词原形

例：只有在这家商店，我们才能买到如此好的家具。

Only in this shop can we buy such good furniture.

例：在1949年战争结束后，他才开始新的生活。

Only when/after the war was over in 1949 was he able to begin a new life.

(2) So＋形容词/副词、Such＋名词位于句首引起的部分倒装

例：他们对哲学了解很少，以至于其中大多数人根本不能理解讲座。

So little did they know about philosophy that the lecture was completely beyond most of them.(beyond sb. 超过某人水平；为某人所不能理解)

例：他是位如此善解人意的人，所以我们都乐意跟他共事。

Such a considerate person is he that we all like to work with him.

29. 祈使句＋and/or＋(含有一般将来时的)陈述句

例：继续努力(再努力一下)，你将来总有一天会成功的。

Keep working hard (Make another effort/Another effort), and you are sure to succeed someday in the future.

例：多吃水果，你就不用担心缺少维生素了。

Eat more fruit, and you don't have to worry about lack of vitamins.

例：听从医生的意见，否则你的咳嗽会更糟糕。

Follow your doctor's advice, or your cough will get worse.

30. not ... but ... 不是……而是……

例：真正重要的不是你所说的，而是你所做的。

It is not what you say but what you do that really counts/matters.

31. Word/News came＋that(同位语)从句 有消息说……

例：消息传来，他已被他向往的大学录取了。

Word/News came that he had been admitted to his ideal university.

32. The reason why/for ... was/is＋that 从句 ……的原因是……

例：他不跟父母说实话的原因是他不想让父母为他担心。(2种句式)

The reason why he didn't tell the truth to his parents was that he didn't want his parents to worry.

The reason for his not telling the truth to his parents was that he didn't want his parents to worry.

33. cannot/can never ... too ... =cannot ... enough 再……也不为过；越……越好

例：第一次独自开车时，你怎么仔细也不为过。

You cannot/can never be too be careful when you drive a car alone for the first time.

例：我对你感激不尽。

I cannot thank you enough.

34. take ... into consideration/account 把……考虑进去；考虑到

例：我希望你们能考虑我给你们提的建议。

I hope that you can take suggestions I gave you into consideration/account.

35. more ... than ... 与其说……倒不如说……

例：经验告诉我们，成功与其说是因为才能，不如说是因为努力工作。

Experience shows that success is due more to hard work than ability.

36. (1) In case+条件状语从句(从句如果用一般现在时，表示的是将来时间；如果用一般过去时，则表示的是过去的将来) 如果，万一

例：如果你需要什么东西，请给我打电话。

In case you need something, please call me.

(2) In case of sth./doing sth. 防备，假如

例：如遇失火，请按警铃。

In case of fire, ring the alarm bell.

37. with+宾语(名词/代词)+宾语补足语(现在分词/过去分词/to do 不定式/形容词/副词/介词短语)

例：在所有的问题都得到解决之后，队长感到很轻松。

With all the problems solved, the team leader felt relaxed.

例：因为今晚有很多作业要做，我不能去参加音乐会。

With so much homework to do in the evening, I can't go to the concert.

例：因为有向导带路，我们没有费多大劲就找到了修理厂。

With the guide leading the way, we had no difficulty in finding the garage.

例：她眼里含着泪水，看着女儿结婚。

With tears of joy in her eyes, she saw her daughter married.

例：由于灯灭了，我们几乎什么也没有看见。

With the lights out, we could hardly see anything.

38. What impressed/struck us most was＋that 从句　最让我们印象深刻的是……

例：最让我们印象深刻的是，无论遇到什么样的困难他永不放弃。

What impressed/struck us most was that he never gave up no matter what difficulties he encountered.

39. With the development/improvement/rise/increase/advance/...　随着……的发展/提高/增长/进步/……

例：随着社会和经济的发展，越来越多来自贫困地区的学生也能受到良好的教育。

With the development of society and economy, more and more students from poor areas can be well-educated.

40. Contrary to one's wish/expectation＝Contrary to what sb. expected/thought　与……相反

例：事与愿违，尽管他训练得很刻苦，他还是在比赛中输了。（2 种句式）

Contrary to his wish/expectation, he lost the game though he trained hard.

Contrary to what he (had) expected/thought, he lost the game though he trained hard.

第四节　写作思维

英语写作与英语学科核心素养中的思维品质密切相关。通过英语写作，我们能够培养和提升思维能力，如逻辑思维、批判性思维和创新性思维等。英语写作要求我们厘清思路并准确表达，这有助于培养我们的逻辑思维；同时，英语写作促使我们多角度地思考问题，这能锻炼我们的批判性思维；另外，在英语写作的创作过程中，我们积极寻求独特的观点，这有助于培养我们的创新性思维。总之,英语写作与思维品质紧密相连、相互促进。以下列举一些在英语写作中能运用到的重要的思维能力。

一、分析思维

分析思维是指通过对问题或现象进行深入思考、剖析其内在的原因以及评估其带来的后果的思维能力。在分析的过程中,我们必须学会抓住问题的关键和核心,迅速找到并解决。在写作时,我们通常会面临大量的信息和细节,需从中提取有用的信息和筛选关键要点,这意味着要运用分析思维抓住问题的本质,辨别对问题影响最大或解决问题最关键的因素。只有明确识别和理解核心要点,才能基于合理的推理和论证做出准确的总结或决策。

如在图表类作文题中,我们经常会面临大量的数据或信息,从中抓取核心问题的过程就是运用分析思维的过程。

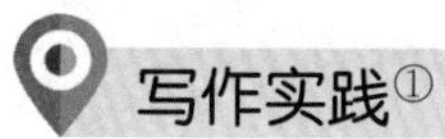

上周你校进行了谁是你的偶像的调查。得出结果如表格所示。请简要描述调查结果,并对此发表自己的看法。

偶　像	男　生	女　生
影视明星	18%	51%
体育明星	48%	7%
科学家、英雄	20%	18%
父母	7%	22%
无偶像	7%	2%

① "写作实践"部分的作文题目来自詹玲:《高考英语写作专项训练》,上海教育出版社,2010,第93页。

学生习作：

As depicted in the table, most students show fancy for idols. Nearly half of the boys are interested in sports stars, whereas over half of the girls are fond of movie stars. More than one-third students admire scientists and heroes. But only seven percent of boys and twenty-two percent of girls choose their parents as their idols.

It's a common phenomenon that we often define idols as those handsome guys or stunning beauties. However, the true meaning of an idol is anyone who inspires you, enlightens you and positively influences your life.

点评

在这个表中，我们可以找到10个数值，但这10个数值必须都写入文章中吗？显然没有必要。我们需要培养学生的分析思维，去解决以下问题：

- 哪些是核心数据？
- 通过这些核心数据，我们可以找到什么核心问题？
- 是什么导致了这个问题？
- 我们应该怎样正确地看待这个问题？/我们应该如何解决这个问题？

通过分析，我们可以得出以下结论：近一半的男生喜欢体育明星(48%)，超过一半的女生喜欢电影明星(51%)。超过三分之一的学生崇拜科学家和英雄(38%)。只有7%的男生和22%的女生选择父母作为他们的偶像。

在这10个数值中，该学生只用了5个数值。通过对比表中的数据，可以得出核心问题：人们常常将偶像定义为那些帅气的男孩或美丽的女孩，但是一个真正的偶像应该是那些鼓励你、启发你并对你生活产生积极影响的人。

可见在写作中，分析思维的重要性：它能够帮助我们在大量的数据和信息中，迅速找到问题的关键所在，从而进行破题；同时，分析思维在后续的原因分析和结果分析中都起着至关重要的作用。

二、逻辑思维

英语写作和逻辑思维密切相关。逻辑思维是指思考问题时清晰地、有条理地推理并进行结构化的能力。在英语写作中，通过逻辑思维可以合理组织论点、提供证据和进行推理，从而让文章具有逻辑性和连贯性。同时，逻辑思维也能够帮助我们识别并纠正文章中的逻辑错误，提高写作的准确性和可信度。

写作实践

> 在对中学生穿校服的情况进行调查之后，写一份调查报告。报告须包含以下内容：
>
> 1. 多数学生赞成：可避免攀比，有利于学校管理；有人反对：设计单调，不利于个性发展。
>
> 2. 谈谈你的看法。

① Recently, I have conducted a survey concerning students' school uniforms. Opinions are divided on this issue, as there are both notable advantages and disadvantages.

② Supporters argue that school uniforms serve as a tradition with several benefits.【主题句】To begin with, wearing the same clothes eliminates the phenomenon for comparison, thus promoting a healthier mindset among students. Furthermore, uniforms provide convenience for school management. Meanwhile, those holding the opposite view maintain that the disadvantages of school uniforms can't be ignored. The monotonous design and colour can make students feel uninterested in wearing them throughout the year.

③ Personally, I believe that the disadvantages outweigh the advantages.【主题句】In the first place, the materials which some school uniforms are made of are often far from comfortable, which may cause physical suffering to students. Worse still, the bland design and colour may have a negative impact on students' aesthetic development. Lastly, wearing school uniforms restricts students' freedom and may hinder the development of their personalities, potentially leading to a lack of creativity.

④ In conclusion, we should relieve the burden of wearing school uniforms on students and allow them more freedom to grow and develop.

点评

一篇优秀的文章，首先需要处理好整篇文章的逻辑关系。此篇文章的结构为总—分—总，文章逻辑清晰。其次，要处理好段内的逻辑关系。在段③中，学生首先表明自己的观点，认为校服的弊大于利；随后，通过 in the first place、worse still、lastly 分述三个理由。尾段④通过 in conclusion 总结全文。

可见，要想把逻辑思维贯彻在写作的过程中，需统筹好宏观和微观之间的关系：既要厘清段落之间的逻辑关系，又要处理好段内的逻辑关系。久而久之，学生的逻辑思维能力一定能得到有效的提升。

三、批判性思维

在英语写作过程中的审题阶段，批判性思维可以帮助我们仔细分析题目要求，理解问题的核心，并促使我们从多个角度进行思考。同时，批判性思维能够帮助我们进行更深层次的思考，客观地评价不同的观点，提出合理的反驳并提供支撑观点的论据。此外，批判性思维还能帮助我们发现逻辑漏洞、错误的假设或论证。因此，批判性思维对于英语写作至关重要。

写作实践

请以“Shopping Online”为题，就网上购物的利弊写一篇作文。

① With the rapid development of science and technology, a good many new things spring up every day. Shopping on the net is just a brand-new way of shopping, which is especially well received by the young. Why does it appeal to so many people? The advantages can be listed as follows.

通过一个问题引出文章的主旨。

② First, shopping on the net does save us a great deal of time.【主题句】We don't have to walk around and around to pick out the things we need. All we need to do is sit before a computer and click the mouse, with a cup of coffee at hand. How convenient and enjoyable it is!

运用主题句引出网上购物的好处。

③ In addition, the net has offered us a wider choice of products, and the prices are comparatively lower.【主题句】Isn't it attractive?

④ However, as each coin has two sides, the disadvantages are also rather apparent. As many people can see, the quality of the products bought on the net is usually not well guaranteed. What's worse/To make things worse, lots of customers have been ripped off while shopping on the net.

阐述网上购物的坏处。

⑤ All things considered/In conclusion/In my opinion, the positive aspects outweigh the negative ones. So, make the choice by

yourself. Whether it is a traditional or fashionable way, both of them can offer us the enjoyment of life.

点评

作者首先列举了网购的几个优势，但在本文段④，笔锋一转，“each coin has two sides”（事物总有两面性），网购一定只有好的一面吗？显然不是，它还有若干的劣势。这就体现了批判性思维。

可见，一篇优秀的高考作文，需要融入批判性思维。我们必须考虑到话题的多个方面，即好的方面和坏的方面；或者主要提及优势，劣势可以一笔带过。反之亦然。

四、创新性思维

写作本身就是一个创新的过程。从语言表达方面来说，创新性思维能够帮助我们以独特和富有创意的方式表达思想，促使我们使用丰富的词汇、多样化的句式和生动的描写来写出引人入胜的文章。创新性思维在写作内容上也能发挥作用，促使我们从不同角度思考问题，提出新颖的见解和独特的观点，并提供创新性的解决方案，从而使我们的作品更富于思想深度和独创性。创新性思维与英语写作相互促进、相互作用。

综上所述，分析思维能够帮助我们把握核心问题，从而分析得出原因和结果；逻辑思维可以帮助我们以合理的结构和清晰的论证来表达观点；批判性思维可以帮助我们多角度地看待同一个问题，审查和评估信息的可靠性和有效性；创新性思维则帮助我们在写作中寻找新颖的观点和方法，使文章更有独特性和吸引力。要想写出一篇优秀的英语作文，我们要学会运用分析思维、逻辑思维、批判性思维和创新性思维等思维能力，并将其体现在自己的文章中。

CHAPTER 02

第二章　教师指导

本书的第一章重点讲述了在高中英语写作教学中，教师要给学生“教什么”。接下来，本章将指导教师该“如何教”，即给教师提供一些在平时的写作教学中可以使用的方法和技巧。

第一节 讲授法

讲授法是英语写作教学中常见的一种方法，其至关重要。

首先，讲授法可以帮助学生系统地学习和掌握写作框架和技巧。通过教师系统的讲解和示范，学生可以了解到词汇、语法、结构等这些构成文章的要素，并习得相应的写作技巧。其次，讲授法是一种循序渐进的指导方法，可以促使学生逐步养成良好的写作习惯，形成规范、清晰和有逻辑的表达方式。

教学实践

教师可以从多种角度来实践讲授法。

1. 按作文文体讲授：见下表。

作文文体	细分			
记叙文	写人		写事	
议论文	图片	图表	现象	选择说理
	利弊	格言、谚语	举例说明	
应用文	建议信	申请信	演讲稿	倡议书

2. 按作文的写作过程讲授：教师可以从学生作文的审题到谋篇布局，再到如何写好主旨句和段落等方面入手，有计划、有序地进行讲授。

3. 按写作技巧讲授：教师在按照作文文体或作文的写作过程讲授时，可以循序渐进地将各种写作技巧如对比法、举例法等渗透其中。

4. 按写作思维讲授：教师在讲授作文的过程中，可渗透各种写作思维，如分析思维、逻辑思维、批判性思维和创新性思维等等。

第二节　以读促写法

以读促写法是一种通过阅读来提高学生英语写作能力的教学方法。学生通过阅读优秀的英语作品，学习其表达技巧和写作风格，从而提高写作水平。

根据苏联著名的心理学家列夫·维果茨基(Lev Vygotsky)的观点，语言和文化是相互关联的，语言是特定社会文化的产物。通过阅读不同领域的英语作品，学习者可以增加词汇量、增长语法知识和提升语境理解能力。此外，美国著名的语言教育家斯蒂芬·克拉申(Stephen D. Krashen)提出的"输入假说"也是以读促写法的理论基石之一。他认为，通过接触大量的、可理解的语言输入，学习者可以逐渐提高他们的语言能力。

以读促写法通过以下三个方面来提升学生的写作能力：

1. 以读促写法对写作语言的提升至关重要。学生通过接触大量的优秀英语作品，学习表达技巧，丰富写作语言。

2. 以读促写法能够帮助学生构建写作结构。学生可以通过阅读各类优秀的英语作品，学习写作的框架，厘清写作思路，组织段落结构。

3. 以读促写法培养学生的写作思维。学生通过阅读，能接触到不同的观点和文化，有助于拓宽视野，提升独立思考能力。

总而言之，以读促写法可以提高学生的写作语言水平，帮助他们构建清晰的写作结构，培养他们的写作思维。与此同时，教师应注重培养学生的阅读习惯，通过指导他们分析和模仿优秀的作品，提升他们的写作水平。

教学实践

教师可以引导学生进行以下具体的阅读活动，以促进写作水平的提高：

1. 阅读大量的优秀英语作品：通过阅读各种文学作品、学术文章等，学生可以接触到不同的思想和风格，能积累丰富的词汇，学习到多样化的表达技巧。

2. 阅读不同种类的图书：除了文学类图书，还可以阅读其他种类的图书，如科学类、历史类、哲学类等，有助于拓宽学生的知识面，增加思考的角度，从而丰富写作内容。

3. 读写结合：在阅读时，可以让学生尝试将所读内容用自己的语言进行概述，写读后感或对文章进行分析和评论等，从而提高学生的理解能力和写作能力。

4. 单元写作：在每学完一个单元后，教师可以有针对性地出一些写作题，让学生将在此单元学到的词汇和语法融入自己的文章，学以致用，以此促进其写作水平的提升。

第三节 头脑风暴法

头脑风暴法作为一种创新性的思维训练方法，在作文教学中具有重要的作用和意义。

教学实践

写作课上，教师可以引导学生从写作语言、写作内容和写作思维三个方面来进行头脑风暴：

1. 鼓励学生利用头脑风暴法大胆地表达思想和观点，丰富写作语言，让作文更生动、具体、有感染力，从而吸引读者的注意力。

2. 头脑风暴法注重延展写作内容的广度和深度，使用该方法时会讨论较多的主题或话题，从而可以培养学生多角度、多元化地看待问题，促进其独立思考，使作文内容更全面。

3. 头脑风暴法有助于培养学生的创新性思维和逻辑思维能力，推动其积极思考，激发其主动创新，增强其思辨意识，从而提升其写作能力。

综上所述，头脑风暴法在作文教学中不仅可以丰富写作语言、写作内容，而且可以培养写作思维，有助于学生写出更加精彩、更有深度的作文。

第四节 分享与展示法

在英语写作教学中，运用分享与展示法非常重要。学生可以在小组中分享自己的写作经验和技巧，并互相借鉴和学习。这种交流和分享可以激发学生的创作激情，提高他们的写作能力。

教学实践

1. 教师可以在课堂上当堂展示优秀文章，并加以点评。

2. 教师也可以在教室划分出一个展示区来展示班级学生的优秀作品。学生通过观摩其他同学的佳作，可以得到借鉴和启发。

3. 教师还可以创建一个英语写作博客或论坛，让学生每周分享一篇自己的作文至平台，并在留言区互动，等等。

4. 教师可以和学生共同甄选一些优秀范文，编成优秀范文集，作为学生学习的材料，同时也可以激发学生写作的积极性。

通过分享与展示法，学生可以相互学习和共同进步，不仅提高了写作能力，而且培养了合作和交流能力。这种方法可以激发学生的学习兴趣和积极性，让英语写作教学变得更加有效和有趣。

第五节 小组合作法

小组合作法是英语写作课中常用的一种教学方法，它通过组织学生进行讨论和交流，促进他们在写作过程中互相学习和协作。

教学实践

1. 组建小组：根据学生的英语水平和兴趣爱好，将学生分成不同的小组。每个小组通常由 3～5 名学生组成，确保小组每个成员都有机会参与讨论和分享自己的观点。

2. 分工合作：在小组中，每个成员可以承担不同的任务——有的负责整理讨论的内容，有的负责查找资料，有的负责撰写草稿，等等。通过分工合作，学生可以提高工作效率和获得学习成果。

3. 讨论和分享：小组成员可以就指定的主题或问题展开讨论。每个成员都可以分享自己的观点和想法，并互相反馈。这样可以促进学生之间的互动和思维碰撞，有助于拓宽写作思路。

4. 合作写作：在小组中，成员们可以共同撰写一篇作文；也可以采用轮流写作的方式，每个人负责写一部分，并在写作过程中进行协商和修改。通过合作写作，可以培养学生的团队合作能力，提升写作技巧。

5. 互相评价：小组成员可以互相阅读和评价彼此的作文。可以对作文的内容、语言、组织结构等提出改进建议和意见。通过互相评价，可以促进学生对自己的写作进行反思，从而提升写作水平。

小组合作法可以为学生提供互相学习和协作的机会，能激发学生的积极性和创造力，有助于学生写作能力和核心素养的提升。

第六节　谈话法

谈话法也叫问答法，是一种有效的写作教学方法。教师与学生通过面对面的沟通、交流，引导学生根据已有的知识、经验，促使其通过独立思考获得新的知识。

教学实践

运用谈话法时，教师应做到以下几点：

1. 做好充分的谈话准备，如拟定谈话提纲。通过向学生提问，了解学生的写作水平和写作需求，适时提供个性化的指导。

2. 提出的写作问题要有启发性，且形式要多样。

3. 问题要具体、明确、难度适宜，符合学生已有的写作知识和经验水平。

4. 教师的提问要面向全体学生，同时给学生留有思考的余地。谈话结束后，应结合学生的问答情况进行小结，指出学生写作中的优缺点。

谈话法在写作教学中具有重要意义，它能够提供个性化的指导和反馈，激发学生的学习兴趣和积极性，帮助他们不断提升自己的写作能力。

第七节　情感渗透法

情感渗透法是教学中一种以情感为主导的教学方式。它强调通过激发学生

的情感、兴趣和情绪，促进他们积极参与学习，提高学习效果。情感渗透法的核心思想是让学生在学习过程中产生情感共鸣，使他们在情感上与所学内容建立联系，增强学习的认同感和意义感。

情感渗透法适用于写作教学且可产生良好的作用。

教学实践

高中学生在刚开始学习英语写作时都会有畏难情绪，教师可以通过以下教学步骤，缓解或消除学生的写作焦虑，提升其写作自信。

1. 营造良好的写作氛围：营造轻松愉快、温馨和谐的学习氛围，让学生感到舒适。

2. 激发情感共鸣：通过引发学生的情感，让他们对写作内容产生浓厚的兴趣和共鸣，增强其写作动力。

3. 运用情境教学：将写作话题带入真实的情境，注重学生的情感体验和情感反应，使学生能从情感体验中获得对知识的深入理解和思考。

4. 培养积极的情感态度：在学习过程中，给予学生鼓励、支持和引导，培养他们积极的情感态度。

5. 情感评价反馈：在作文评价与反馈中，注重肯定和激励学生的情感表现，使学生在情感上得到认同和成长。

通过将情感渗透法运用于写作教学，教师可以增强学生的学习情感体验，提高学生学习的主动性和积极性，从而促进学生的发展和成长。

第八节　思维导图法

思维导图法是一种有助于整理思路和构建逻辑关系的写作方法。通过列出主题，并用分支连接相关的子主题或论点，帮助我们清晰地组织和呈现文章的结构。经常使用思维导图法，能够使写作过程更加有序、清晰，能够提高文章的逻辑性和可读性。当然，思维导图法还可以用于拓展写作内容、丰富写作语言及明晰写作评价等各个方面。

教学实践

以黄浦区2023届高三一模作文题为例进行写作教学设计。本次写作话题是“云课堂与建议”，写作目的是让学生复习建议信。在写前的头脑风暴中，学生先构建了建议信的基本框架结构图，见图1。

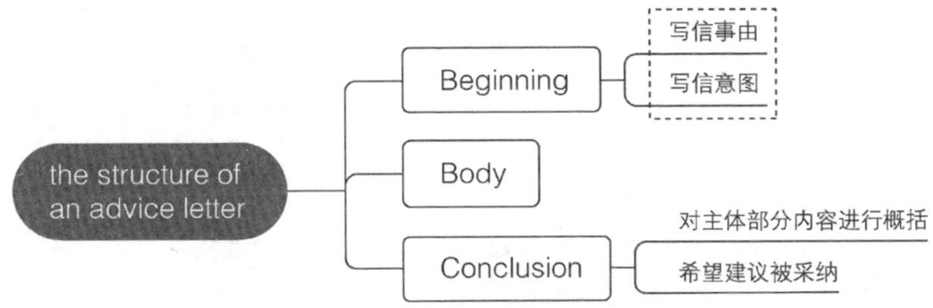

图1 建议信的基本框架结构

通过全班头脑风暴，在已有的思维导图基础上，进一步提取学生已有的相关语言，见图2。

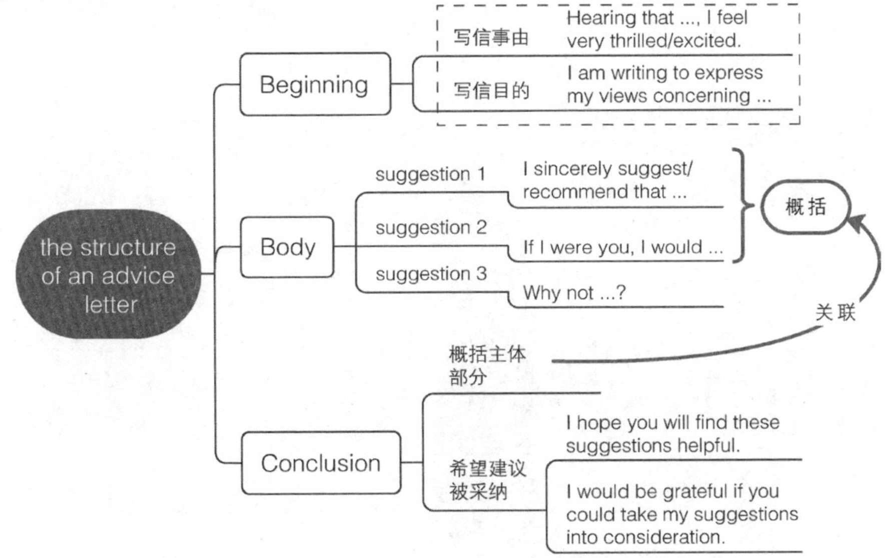

图2 建议信常用句型

接下来，在小组合作中，学生产出了主体部分的框架结构，见图3。

经过课堂写作，最后进入写后环节。教师给学生呈现思维导图形式的评价量表，引导学生自评和互评，相互借鉴，提升写作能力，见图4。

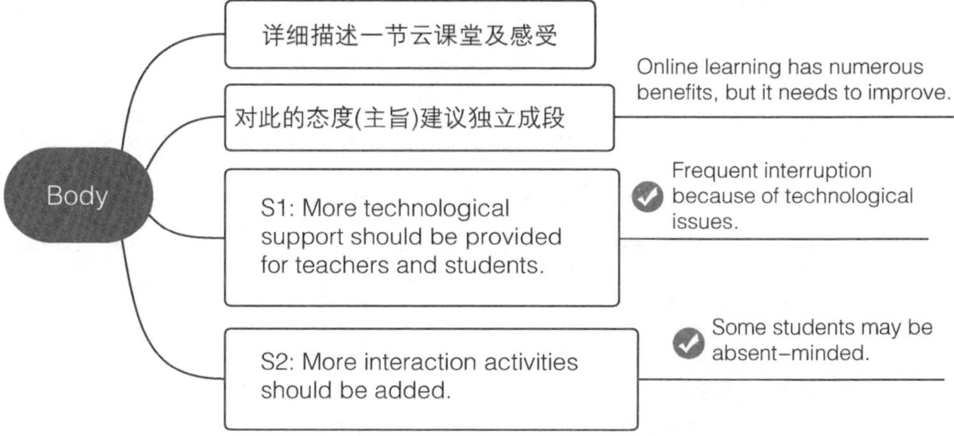

图 3　主体部分的框架结构(某小组的合作成果)

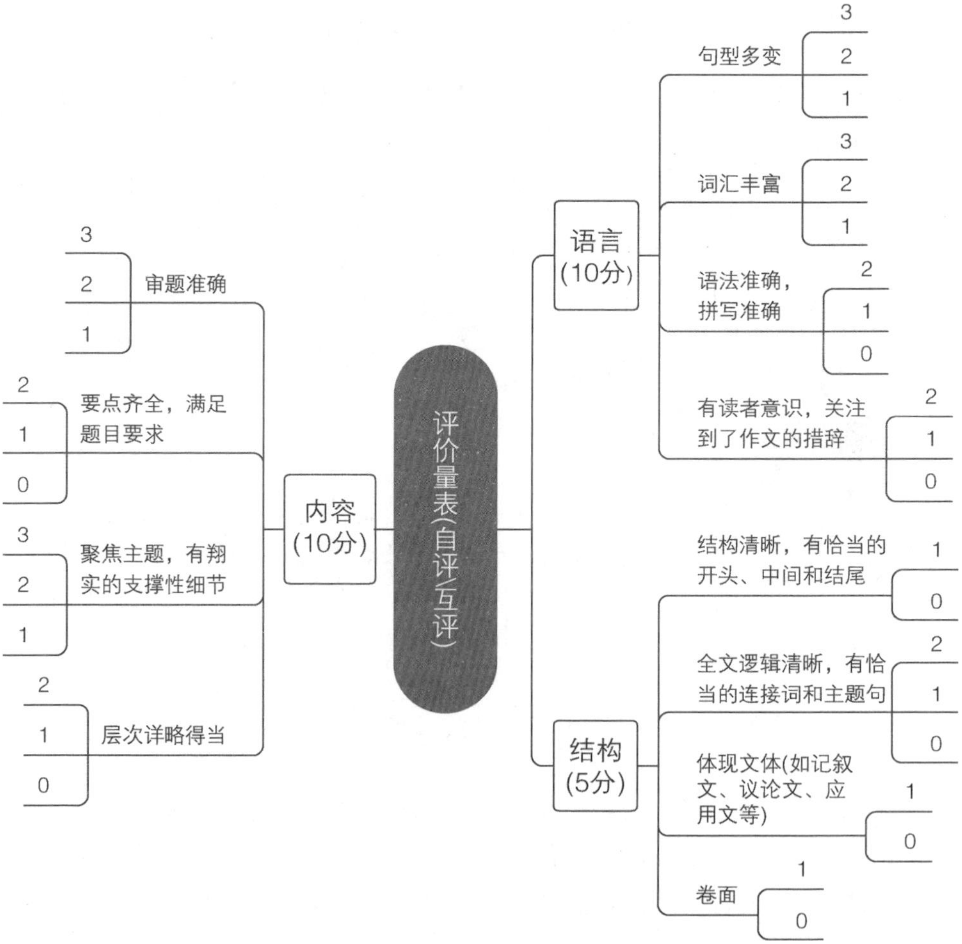

评价量表(自评/互评)

- 内容(10分)
  - 审题准确：3 / 2 / 1
  - 要点齐全，满足题目要求：2 / 1 / 0
  - 聚焦主题，有翔实的支撑性细节：3 / 2 / 1
  - 层次详略得当：2 / 1 / 0
- 语言(10分)
  - 句型多变：3 / 2 / 1
  - 词汇丰富：3 / 2 / 1
  - 语法准确，拼写准确：2 / 1 / 0
  - 有读者意识，关注到了作文的措辞：2 / 1 / 0
- 结构(5分)
  - 结构清晰，有恰当的开头、中间和结尾：1 / 0
  - 全文逻辑清晰，有恰当的连接词和主题句：2 / 1 / 0
  - 体现文体(如记叙文、议论文、应用文等)：1 / 0
  - 卷面：1 / 0

图 4　思维导图形式的评价量表

通过这四个思维导图，学生不仅明晰了写作的结构，也掌握了写作的内容、语言以及评价标准。这样大多数学生就能比较容易地写出一篇不错的作文了。

第九节　档 案 袋 法

档案袋法运用在写作教学中，效果也是非常不错的。

教学实践

从学习写作开始，教师可以引导学生在档案袋中放入以下内容：

1. 优秀习作。教师可以引导学生把平时的优秀习作放入自己专属的写作档案袋。这些习作可以是经过学生反复精修的文章，上面有教师的评分和评语；也可以是其他同学的优秀作品，可以用来模仿和借鉴。

2. 好词好句。学生应该准备一本好词好句的摘抄本，这也是这个档案袋的重要组成部分。A 档的高考作文要求学生有丰富的词汇和多变的句型储备，“罗马非一日建成”，需要学生日积月累。

3. 主题词汇。英语写作需要有充实的内容、丰富的语言。在阐述一个话题时，学生需要有足够的主题词汇，才能够在高考的短时间内下笔如有神。因此，学生应该做一个有心人，通过日常的课文学习、课后练习或报刊阅读去积累主题词汇，这样才能在正式写作时做到“手中有粮”。

教师将以上九种写作教学方法合理运用于自己的教学课堂，一定会对自身的写作教学有所帮助。

CHAPTER 03

第三章　教学评价

第一节　写作教学评价的分类

第二节　写作教、学、评一体化的实施

第三节　写作教、学、评一体化的实施特点

第四节　写作评价工具的设计和应用

《普通高中英语课程标准(2017 年版 2020 年修订)》提出建立以学生为主体,促进学生全面、健康而有个性地发展的课程评价体系,要求"教师应处理好评价与教和学之间的关系,推动教、学、评一体化实施"。因此,教师在整个教学流程中,要以教学目标为引领、以教学评价为导向,让教师的教、学生的学、教学的评协同配合,构建一个完整、高效的课堂教学体系。作为高中英语的重要组成部分,写作也应该深度融入教、学、评一体化的理念。

第一节　写作教学评价的分类

传统的教学评价往往只关注学习结果,即考试成绩,评价被简化为测试,导致考试的功能和作用被片面夸大。开展教、学、评一体化就是要凸显以评促学、以评促教的功能,这将引导教师更加关注教学过程中学生主动参与的态度、学习投入的程度以及实际的学习成效,从而通过学生的即时反馈来调整教学策略,确保教学目标的实现。

教学评价一般可以分成安置性评价、形成性评价、阶段性评价和终结性评价,写作教学评价同样可以分为此四大类。

1. 写作安置性评价

写作安置性评价是指在写作教学的准备阶段,对学生学情、教学内容和任务设计三方面进行评价,从而帮助教师调整备课内容和提高专业能力。

王蔷、李亮将教、学、评一体化系统归纳为明确理念、把握内容、分析学情、制定目标、选择方法、评价效果等要素和环节,具体如图 1 所示。

在"分析学情"的过程中,教师就需要用到安置性评价。通过问卷调查、访谈、测评等多种形式去评估学生在所学内容、已有的知识、经验、能力和态度以及潜在不足等方面的总体表现,判断学生的起点,为后面的"制定目标"提供有力的支撑和方向。

2. 写作形成性评价

写作形成性评价是指通过课堂的即时反馈或课后的反馈和指导,来帮助学习者逐步提升写作能力和技巧的评价。其强调过程中的反思和改进、学生的自主学习和成长。以下为写作形成性评价的分类:

（1）教师口头评价：指教师在课堂内对学生在学习过程中表现出来的能力和进展进行即时的口头反馈。在王蔷、李亮的“教、学、评一体化设计与实施的相关要素分析”（图 1）的最后一个环节“评价效果”中，教师应根据学生的课堂表现，根据目标达成，发现问题、给出反馈、做出调整。

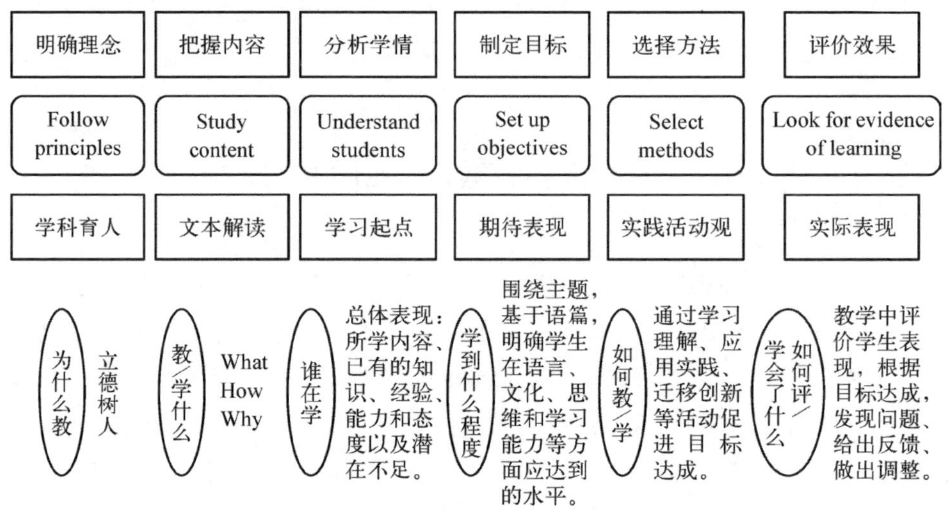

图 1　教、学、评一体化设计与实施的相关要素分析①

（2）教师作业评价：指教师对学生在完成作业的过程中展现出来的学习能力和知识掌握情况进行的评价。在图 1 的所有环节结束后，教师布置写作任务，通过批改评价，发现问题，并指导学生进行调整。作业评价是形成性评价的重要组成部分，这就要求作业的评价标准不能过于单一。对于多样性的作业，教师应该有多种评价方式，尽量以具有指导性、鼓励性的评价引导学生进行调整，帮助学生建立自信和提升学习能力。

（3）学生自评：指学生在写作过程中，根据教师提供的写作评价标准对自己的作品进行评价、反思和修正，以提高写作能力和增强自我意识。

（4）学生互评：指学生根据教师所给的评价量表对彼此学习过程中的表现和进展进行评价。通过对同伴的评价，学生可以相互学习、互相启发，同时也能够更好地了解自己的学习情况。（见表 1）

---

① 王蔷、李亮：《推动核心素养背景下英语课堂教—学—评一体化：意义、理论与方法》，《课程・教材・教法》2019 年第 5 期。

表 1 学生作文评价量表(自评/互评)

	标准描述	得分				
内容(10 分)		三档(4 分)	二档(2 分)	一档(0 分)		
	1. 审题准确。					
		五档(2 分)	四档(1.5 分)	三档(1 分)	二档(0.5 分)	一档(0 分)
	2. 要点齐全,满足题目要求。					
	3. 聚焦主题且有翔实的支撑性材料/细节。					
	4. 层次详略得当。					
语言(10 分)	1. 句型变化多样且得体有效。					
	2. 用词丰富得当,有一定的超纲词汇。					
	3. 语法结构正确,只有少数语法错误。					
	4. 运用了恰当的衔接手法,行文流畅,有自己的语言风格。					
	5. 没有拼写、标点和大小写错误。					
结构(5 分)		三档(1 分)	二档(0.5 分)	一档(0 分)		
	1. 有恰当的开头、中间和结尾。					
	2. 分段合理且有清晰的主题句和过渡句。					
	3. 段落之间和段落内部整体连贯,逻辑合理。					
	4. 体现文体(如记叙文、议论文、应用文等)。					
	5. 卷面整洁。					
总分:						

续　表

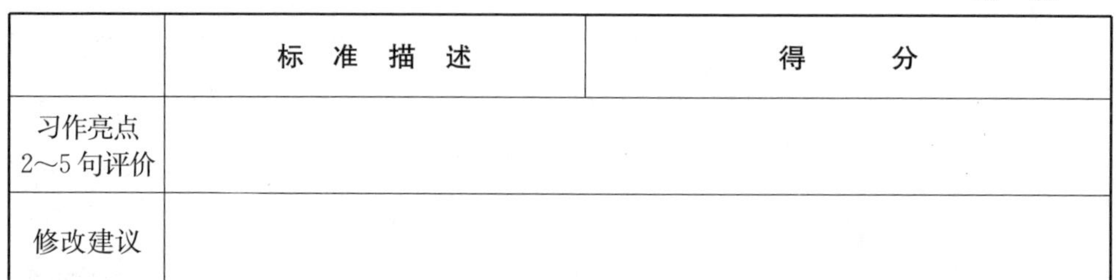

	标　准　描　述	得　　分
习作亮点 2~5 句评价		
修改建议		

3. 写作阶段性评价

写作阶段性评价是指对学生在某个特定写作学习阶段中所达到的学习目标和表现进行的综合评价。其能调整教师的写作教学策略，促进学生写作水平的提高。

如教师可以在教完议论文中的图片类作文后，有针对性地出一些类似的作文题目，对学生进行阶段性测评。当然，阶段性评价也可以在月考中体现，如对整个议论文部分进行复习。总之，阶段性评价可以是小阶段也可以是大阶段的，可以是学生访谈、问卷也可以是阶段性测试，等等。之所以利用多种形式相结合的评价方式，其目的就是要发现学生的问题，为教师提供教学方向。

4. 写作终结性评价

写作终结性评价是在写作结束后对学生的总体写作表现进行的评价，旨在评估和总结学生的写作能力和进步程度。

每个学段较为重要的测试可以称为终结性评价，如期末考试或高考等。上海的英语高考改革对于写作能力的评价可以分为写作测试和口头表达两种，体现在笔头测试的作文部分和听说测试的看图说话部分（即一篇口头小作文）。因此，建议教师在高一至高三各个学段，均可采用将写作测试和口头表达两种方式相结合的终结性评价方式。

第二节　写作教、学、评一体化的实施

实施写作教、学、评一体化的过程包括确定教学目标与评价标准、设计综合写作课程、引导学生进行实践写作活动、提供有针对性的反馈与指导、评价学生的写作成果、根据评价结果对课程进行调整与改进，以促进学生写作能力的全面发展。我们可以把具体实施阶段分成课前、课中和课后三个阶段。

1. 课前

教师开展写作教学和评价活动时要让学生充分参与其中。在进行写作安置性评价时，要以学生为中心，以解决问题为导向，通过教学内容和学习活动落实既定的教学目标。

2. 课中

首先，教师要用提问、观察、布置表现性任务等方式实施互动评价，实时监测学生的表现，确定学生当前水平与期待水平或潜在水平之间的差距，向学生提供支架，及时地给予学生反馈，帮助学生取得更大的进步。其次，在开展评价活动时，教师不仅要说明活动的内容和形式，还应给出活动的要求和评价标准，使学生了解明确的目标，并能根据标准进行自评和互评。最后，教师要鼓励学生参与评价标准的协商与制定，使他们从评价的接受者转变为评价活动的主体和积极参与者，从而有效地调控自己的学习进程并从中获得成就感和自信心。

3. 课后

课后的反思阶段，教师要评价课堂效果，反思并做出调整，为日后的教学改进或“补救”做足准备。在学生的学习结束后，教师要通过课后练习、课后作业、单元测验、学生反思、师生面谈等方式考查学生知识的增长、经验的丰富、能力的提升和态度的转变等情况，全面评价学生在语言能力、思维品质、文化意识和学习能力四个方面的发展变化。(见图 2)

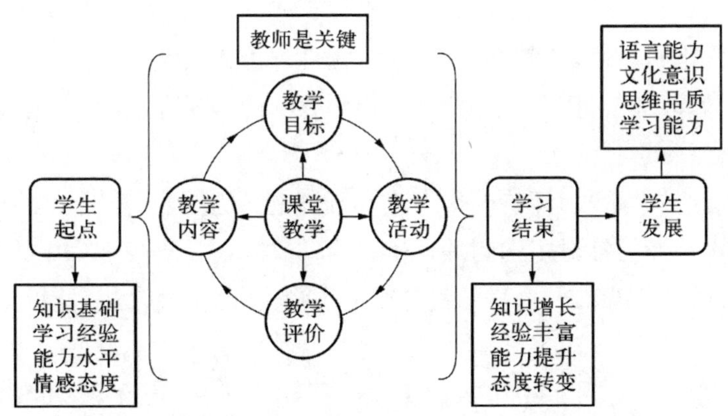

图 2 教、学、评一体化设计与实施的育人系统工程图①

① 王蔷、李亮：《推动核心素养背景下英语课堂教—学—评一体化：意义、理论与方法》,《课程·教材·教法》2019 年第 5 期。

第三节　写作教、学、评一体化的实施特点

《普通高中英语课程标准(2017年版2020年修订)》强调,普通高中英语课程应建立以学生为主体,促进学生全面、健康而有个性地发展的课程评价体系。教师授课时应采用形成性评价和终结性评价相结合的多元评价方式,重视评价的促学作用。因此,写作教学必须加强"以学生为主体"的评价方式,提升学生的自我反思、写作与学习能力。

1. 评价的主体是学生

学生是学习和评价的主体。在写作教学过程中,教师应积极引导学生参与讨论,共同确定评价的目标、内容和形式。此外,教师还应帮助学生掌握科学的评价方法和工具,推动他们进行自评和互评,以此来提高学生的自我反思、调控和修正能力。通过这样的方式,学生之间可以加强交流与合作,共同取得进步。

同时,学生也需积极参与到评价标准的讨论和制定中,参与自评和互评,主动发现、分析和修正写作中的问题。这样才能真正把握写作的核心要点,熟练掌握写作技巧,感受语言的魅力,从而发挥好"以评促学"的作用。

2. 评价应贯穿于写作教学的全过程

在"以学生为主体"的教学理念下,过程性评价应贯穿于写作的全过程,包括构思、草稿、修改和校订等阶段,使评价成为教学的重要环节,有效地推动各阶段的教学进展。

针对不同教学阶段,评价的重点应有所侧重。例如,在教授学生如何撰写主题句后,可设计专门针对主题句的评价工具;同样,在完成段落写作的教学后,也可制定相应的评价标准。这样的设计有助于学生在各个阶段都能得到有针对性的反馈和指导。

教师在学生写作过程中应密切关注其存在的问题,并给予及时的提示和关注。在修改阶段,主要评价学生的初稿是否符合写作要求,通过评价找出问题并指导学生进行修正。在编辑阶段,则通过评价工具,引导学生自我检查并修正语法、标点、拼写等错误。

完成整篇文章后，师生可参照高考写作评分标准，共同制定评价量表。通过学生的自评和互评，不仅可以提高评价的有效性，更能促进教学和学习质量的提升，实现评价与教学的良性互动。

第四节 写作评价工具的设计和应用

评价工具可辅助教师实施“以学生为主体”的评价方式。教师应结合写作的教学目标、内容、要求和学生的学习水平等情况，与学生共同制定实用的评价标准，并选择适用于写作教学不同阶段的教育评价工具。以下是几种常用的评价工具。

1. 检查列表

检查列表的设计要点应该根据不同的写作文体、写作要求和写作内容而有所不同。

如记叙文，可分成计划构思、拟写草稿、修改文稿和编辑校订四个写作阶段。以计划构思阶段为例，可以设计一个检查列表，旨在帮助学生明确写作思路。这份列表应涵盖确定写作主题、搜集相关素材、精心选择内容以及确定文章组织方式等关键步骤。通过这份列表，学生能够更好地理解和掌握记叙文的写作要点，为后续拟写草稿和修改文稿奠定坚实的基础。以下是一个计划构思阶段的检查列表，教师可根据实际情况进行调整：

Checklist for Planning

☐ What topic do you want to focus on?

☐ What is the thesis statement of your writing?

☐ What are the main events and characters involved in your writing?

☐ How are you going to arrange and organize your writing?

☐ What feelings do you want to express through your writing?

通过这份检查列表，学生可以逐项检查自己的计划构思是否完善，并在必要时进行调整和补充。这将有助于他们后续的写作过程更加有条不紊地展开，提高文章的质量和完整性。同时，教师也可以根据这份列表给予学生有针

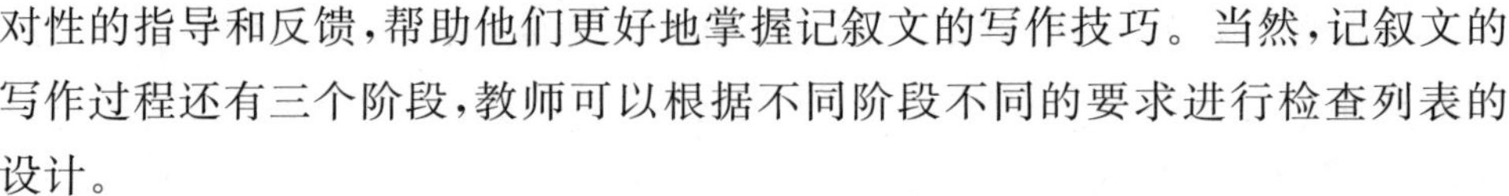

对性的指导和反馈，帮助他们更好地掌握记叙文的写作技巧。当然，记叙文的写作过程还有三个阶段，教师可以根据不同阶段不同的要求进行检查列表的设计。

再如，一个清晰、有条理的结构可以构成一个好的段落，好的段落又对表达思想至关重要。一个典型的段落通常由三个部分组成：主题句、支持句和总结句。主题句是段落的首句，通常明确阐述该段落的核心观点或主题。它是对整个段落内容的预览和概括，为读者理解接下来的内容提供线索。支持句紧随主题句之后，通过具体的例子、事实、分析或推理来详细解释和支撑主题句中的观点。这些句子应紧密围绕主题展开，确保段落的连贯性和一致性。总结句为段落的尾句，对整个段落的内容进行简短的回顾和总结，有时也会对主题进行升华或提出进一步的思考。总结句有助于加强读者对段落主题的印象，并为可能的后续段落做铺垫。教师可以设计以下检查列表：

Checklist for Paragraph Organization：

□ Does the opening sentence clearly state the central idea of the paragraph?

□ Do the subsequent sentences provide relevant examples and details that directly support the topic sentence?

□ Is there a logical and coherent flow between the sentences in the paragraph?

□ Does the final sentence effectively conclude the paragraph, summarizing the main points or leaving a lasting impression?

这个检查列表不仅是学生提升自我写作能力的有效工具，也是教师指导学生写作的重要参考。通过逐一检查列表中的每个问题，学生可以清晰地认识到自己在段落组织方面的不足之处，从而有针对性地进行改进。教师也可以通过这个检查列表来评估学生的写作水平，发现普遍存在的问题，进而调整教学策略，提高教学效果。这种以评促学、以评促教的方式，有助于培养学生的写作思维，提升他们的写作能力，同时也促进了教师教学水平的提升，实现了教学相长的良好循环。

2. 评价量表

评价量表是判断与评价学生写作的标准或规则。评价量表可以帮助学生在写作前做好准备工作，引导学生在拟写草稿、修改文稿等阶段进行自我评价和改进，适用于写作过程中的各个阶段。

写作教材 *Write Source* 指出，评价量表是评定写作等级的量表。评价量表可以从观点(ideas)、布局结构(organization)、风格(voice)、用词(word choice)、句子流畅度(sentence fluency)和标准(conventions)等六大要素对写作进行评价。评价等级分为六等，分别是 6(amazing)、5(strong)、4(good)、3(okay)、2(poor)、1(incomplete)。师生可以根据每一个等级的相关文字描述对写作的六大要素进行评价。以下是议论文写作的评价量表：

特点(Traits)	**分数(Grades)**					
	6	**5**	**4**	**3**	**2**	**1**
观点(ideas)						
布局结构(organization)						
风格(voice)						
用词(word choice)						
句子流畅度(sentence fluency)						
标准(conventions)						

以上表中关于观点(ideas)的评价为例，我们可以看到这样的等级描述：

Grade 6：The writer's opinion is very well defended and firmly convinces the reader.

Grade 5：The writing has a clear opinion statement and persuasive details to support the writer's opinion.

Grade 4：The opinion statement is clear and has most details to support the writer's opinion.

Grade 3：The opinion statement is clear but more persuasive details are needed to support the writer's opinion.

Grade 2：The opinion statement is clear and persuasive details are needed.

Grade 1：A new opinion statement and supporting details are needed.

再如，根据上海高考作文的评分细则并结合课堂实际，教师可以设计形式如下的思维导图式评价量表：

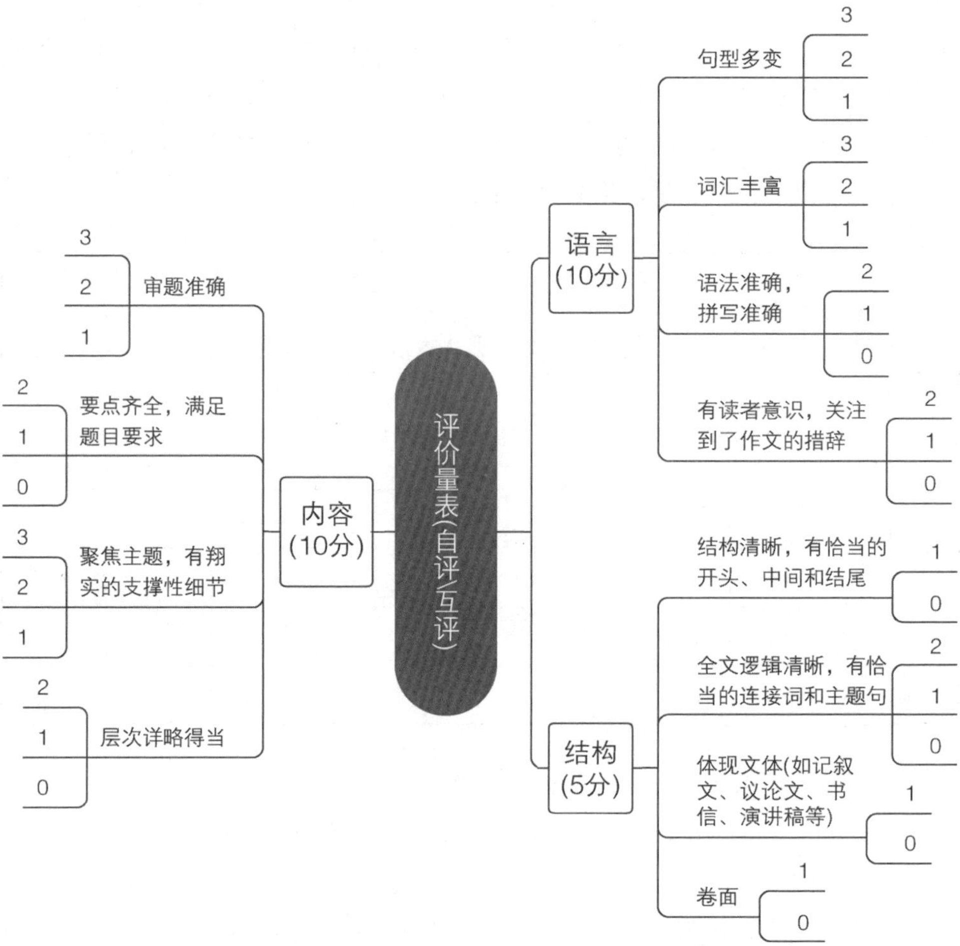

- 评价量表(自评/互评)
  - 内容(10分)
    - 审题准确：3 / 2 / 1
    - 要点齐全，满足题目要求：2 / 1 / 0
    - 聚焦主题，有翔实的支撑性细节：3 / 2 / 1
    - 层次详略得当：2 / 1 / 0
  - 语言(10分)
    - 句型多变：3 / 2 / 1
    - 词汇丰富：3 / 2 / 1
    - 语法准确，拼写准确：2 / 1 / 0
    - 有读者意识，关注到了作文的措辞：2 / 1 / 0
  - 结构(5分)
    - 结构清晰，有恰当的开头、中间和结尾：1 / 0
    - 全文逻辑清晰，有恰当的连接词和主题句：2 / 1 / 0
    - 体现文体(如记叙文、议论文、书信、演讲稿等)：1 / 0
    - 卷面：1 / 0

图 3　思维导图形式的评价量表

师生通过评价量表具体、清晰的文字描述，可以准确地判断一篇文章的等级。全面、清晰的评价内容和标准，使教师在批阅作文时能高效地发现学生写作中存在的问题，并据此提出有针对性的指导意见。学生也可以利用这一量表进行自我评价和同伴互评，从而更好地修改自己的写作，提升写作水平。

针对不同写作文体，评价量表的内容和特征需要进行相应的调整。例如，议论文的评价量表可能更注重论点的明确性、论据的充分性、论证的逻辑性等方面的评价；而记叙文的评价量表可能更注重故事情节的完整性、人物形象的生动性、语言表达的感染力等方面的评价;等等。

当然,除了这些评价工具外,教师也可直接通过口头或书面的方式进行评价。通过口头或书面的交流沟通,对学生写作中的问题加以具体指导,对学生的点滴进步给予鼓励,激励他们学习写作的积极性和主动性,帮助他们树立信心,切实提升英语写作水平。

教、学、评一体化的写作教学方法旨在引导教师将注意力从仅关注写作教学结果转向同时关注写作教学的结果和学习过程,以教学、学习和评价三个方面的一致性,有效地打造高效的写作课堂。然而,要实施写作教学的教、学、评一体化,教师首先需要对写作教学目标有清晰的理解;此外,评价方法在教学的各个环节中的适当应用是实现一体化的关键。相信通过深度融合上述提到的各种评价方式,教师能够显著提升教学效果。

CHAPTER 04

第四章　写作教学的课堂案例

第一节　写作教学的基本流程

英语写作课有多种多样的形式，但是每一种形式都有一个基本的流程框架：

1. 导入活动：引入写作主题，激发学生的写作兴趣。可以使用图片、视频、故事等来引入写作主题，并与学生进行讨论，启发他们进行思考和表达。

2. 提供语言材料：根据写作主题，提供相关的语言材料，如词汇、短语、句型等。可以通过阅读文章、听力材料等方式来呈现语言材料，帮助学生增加词汇量和语法知识。

3. 撰写文章大纲：根据写作类型，帮助学生撰写写作大纲。大纲包括引言、主体段落和结论，每个部分都需要有明确的主题句和支撑细节。教师可以通过示范写作大纲的方式来帮助学生理解和掌握写作结构。

4. 模仿写作：让学生参考写作材料，进行模仿写作。教师可以向学生展示范文，并解析范文的组织结构、语言运用等要点，引导学生学习和模仿。学生可根据自己的理解和思考来完成模仿写作。

5. 小组讨论和修改：学生完成模仿写作后，进行集体讨论和修改。通过互相交流和反馈，帮助彼此改善写作。教师可以指导学生如何提出具体的修改意见，并解释修改的原因和可能达到的效果。

6. 个别化辅导和反馈：根据学生的写作情况，对有需要的学生进行个别化的辅导和反馈。教师可以安排个别化会议或组织写作指导小组，以提供具体的写作建议，帮助学生进一步提高写作水平。

7. 写作展示：在课堂快结束时，让学生进行写作展示。学生可以朗读自己的写作作品，或进行展示性演讲。通过展示，学生可以互相学习和借鉴他人的写作技巧和思路，进一步提高写作能力。

通过以上教学设计流程，可以激发学生的写作兴趣，培养他们的写作能力，提高他们的英语语言表达水平，同时也能够让学生在写作中培养独特的思维能力。

第二节　写作教学的课堂案例分析

案例 1

英语学习活动观视域下的写作教学实践分析
——“促进英语写作语言表达多样性”案例

【摘　要】 课程标准提出整合英语课堂内容的六个要素，以发展学生的英语学科核心素养为具体目标。在英语写作教学中，提升教学效果是每位英语教师亟待解决的问题。本文先阐述了英语学习活动观的含义，然后以写作展示课为例，说明了如何以发展学生的英语核心素养为目标，在英语学习活动观的帮助下，展示语言风格的多样性，提升学生的写作能力，并促进学生核心素养的转化。

【关键词】 高中写作教学；英语学习活动观；语言表达；核心素养

一、英语学习活动观的内涵

《普通高中英语课程标准(2017 年版 2020 年修订)》(本文以下简称“课程标准”)对英语学习活动观的内涵进行了定义，是指学生在主题意义引领下，通过学习理解、应用实践、迁移创新等一系列体现综合性、关联性和实践性等特点的英语学习活动，使学生基于已有的知识，依托不同类型的语篇，在分析问题和解决问题的过程中，促进自身语言知识学习、语言技能发展、文化内涵理解、多元思维发展、价值取向判断和学习策略运用。这个过程既有助于语言知识和技能的整合发展，也能够不断增强文化意识、提升思维品质和学习能力。

二、基于英语学习活动观的高中英语写作教学设计

基于英语学习活动观，笔者设计了一堂高三英语写作展示课，主题为“家国情怀”。学生需要通过运用他们所学的英语语言表达多样性的技巧，对已经写好的关于“母爱”的作文进行二次加工，以提高他们的语言运用能力。

(一) 教学内容

本节课是“语言表达多样性写作专题”的第三节课。在前两节课中，学生学

习了如何使用定语从句、名词性从句、状语从句、强调句、倒装句、非谓语以及修辞手法等相关技巧。本节课将从学生之前写的一篇关于母爱的作文入手，通过修改作文，来准确把握学生的典型问题，了解学生的学情。根据学生的学情，笔者设计了多种课堂任务和小组活动，包括学习语言表达多样性的实例，引导学生进行实践应用；同时进行小组分层教学，让学生合作完成润色、修饰作文的任务。在课堂上，通过现场写作，鼓励学生进行迁移创新实践，以实现所学知识的内化。通过以上各种形式的活动，培养学生自主学习和合作学习的意识，提升他们的语言表达多样性。

（二）学情分析

本节课的教学对象为高三第一学期某市重点学校平行班的学生，学生英语水平中等，基本能熟练运用英语表达思想。但是在“语言表达多样性写作专题”的第二节课中，通过批改学生写的关于母爱的作文，发现学生的语言表达方式比较单一，根据第二节课的学情，笔者制定了本节课的教学目标。

（三）教学目标

本节课的教学目标是让学生实现在学习理解、应用实践、迁移创新三个层次上的提升，培养他们对写作内容进行探究的能力和核心素养。

1. 掌握语言表达多样性的技巧，如名词性从句、定语从句、倒装句、非谓语和修辞手法等。

2. 在小组合作中完成文章的润色任务，提升学生内化语言表达多样性的技巧的能力。

3. 运用所学的语言表达多样性的技巧，表达对祖国母亲的爱意并献上祝福，回归主题。

三、基于英语学习活动观的高中英语写作教学实践

本节课以“家国情怀”为主题，采用读、译、改、评结合的形式开展教学。

（一）创设情境，激活背景知识

建构主义认为，学习总是与一定的社会文化背景相联系的。因此，在写作课堂中，笔者展示了热门电影《我和我的祖国》的海报和两个版本的英文简介，以营造轻松、愉悦的学习氛围。接下来，学生需要进行学习理解、应用实践和迁移创新的学习活动。笔者要求学生在阅读完两个版本的英文简介后，选择其认为较

好的一篇并阐述原因。这样的学习活动可以帮助学生利用自身认知结构中的经验，将新知识与已有知识联系起来，从而使学习更有意义。通过以上教学，可以激发学生的学习兴趣，提高学习效率，并培养他们在实际情境中运用英语写作的能力。

T：After you read the two versions of the introduction to *My Country, My People*, which one do you like better? Tell me why.

S1：The second one. Because its language is more varied.

S2：The second one. Because the language is brief and more vivid.

T：Exactly. The brief and vivid language can help improve the diversity of the language expression in the second version.

当学生沉浸在快乐的学习氛围中时，笔者又要求学生回忆："What are the skills for the diversity of the language expression that we've learned last class?"（见图 1）

What are the skills for the diversity of the language expression that we've learned last class?

↓

S1：Noun clause，attributive clause.
S2：Inversion，non-predicate.
S3：Figures of speech.

图 1

笔者带领学生一起归纳总结前面课堂上学习的语言表达多样性的技巧，为接下来的相关训练做有效铺垫。（见图 2）

Writing skills for the diversity of the language expression：

Noun clause
Attributive clause
Inversion
Non-predicate
Figures of speech

图 2

笔者在这个阶段充分激发了学生的学习兴趣,提高了学生参与课堂发言的积极性,有助于学生自主发现和探究问题,符合学生的认知规律。

(二) 应用实践,培养语言能力

在实践过程中,培养学生的语言能力也非常重要。根据课程标准的定义,语言能力是指在社会情境中,以听、说、读、看、写等方式理解和表达意义的能力,以及在学习和使用语言的过程中形成的语言意识和语感。这种能力是构成英语学科核心素养的基本要素。在这节课中,笔者通过导入部分让学生回顾了前两节课学过的英语语言表达多样性的技巧;紧接着,笔者要求学生运用技巧进行有针对性的练习。一开始,笔者要求学生写一封信给自己的母亲,表达对母亲的爱和感恩之情。在修改学生作文时,笔者挑选出写得比较好的句子,并给出中文翻译,然后再要求学生将笔者提供的中文翻译用以上归纳的语言表达多样性的技巧进行表达,以加强其英语写作意识和语言技能。(见图 3 和图 4)

句 1 你就像散发光芒的太阳,你的拥抱像是为我遮风的伞,你的声音像是灌溉我心灵的雨水。(protect; water)(明喻;现在分词做后置定语)

图 3

句 2 正如谚语说的那样,生活不是一帆风顺的,学习也是如此,你应当铭记在心。因此,面对困难时,你绝对不能对自己失去信心。(nor; when)(倒装句+定语从句+非谓语)

图 4

在进行了简单的句子实践后,笔者会提供一篇需要润色的作文,要求学生诊断作文存在的问题,并完成润色任务。润色作文的任务以小组的形式展开,课前会根据润色任务的难易程度、学生的学习情况和能力进行分组,并要求学生以小组为单位进行讨论和修改。同时,笔者还设计了“信封救援”活动,旨在帮助那些学习困难的学生,给他们提供自主学习的机会,让他们通过查看信封中的建议,来拓宽润色作文的思路。(见图 5 至图 7)

Groups 1、4

How time flies! I know that the annual Mother's Day is around the corner. I prepare a letter to express my thanks and love to you. I want to tell you something in my deep heart and the things are as follows:

修改建议:

① 将首段的第二、第三两句整合成一句,用分词形式进行修改;

② 将第四句用主语从句表达。

小组修改稿:

How time flies! Knowing that the annual Mother's Day is around the corner, I prepare a letter to express may thanks and love to you. What I want to tell you in my deep heart are as follows.

图 5

Groups 2、5

From my perspective, you are like an umbrella. You protect me through my whole life and shelter me from the wind and rain when I was bullied by others. And this makes me become a courageous person.

Besides, you show me the way clearly and told me that "Life is no plain sailing, nor is learning" which I will remember forever. Your encouragement made me confident and believe that I can overcome the frustration in my study and even in life.

修改建议:

① 第一段的第一、第二句可以合并,用分词做伴随状语的形式进行修改;

② 第一段的第三句可用非限制性定语从句修改;

③ 第二段的首句请用明喻这一修辞手法,可改为"你像为我指明方向的灯塔";

④ 第二段的第二句可用一个同位语从句进行修改。

小组修改稿:

From my perspective, you are like an umbrella, protecting me through my whole life and shelter me form the wind and rain when I was bullied by others, which makes me become a courageous person.

You are like a beacon pointing my way, telling me "Life is no plain sailing, nor is learning", which I will remember forever. Your encouragement made me confident and hold a firm belief that I can overcome the frustration in my study and even in life.

图 6

Groups 3、6

So I am here to thank you, my dear mum. Thank you for your love. You not only protect me but also enlighten me. Your love can help me overcome every difficulty I meet with. I will love you forever!

修改建议：

① 末段的第一、第二句可整合成一句话，用 for 直接表原因；

② 可将第三句中的 not only 提前，用倒装句来修改；

③ 可将第四句改写成强调句。

小组修改稿：

So I am here to thank you, my dear mum for your deep love. Not only do you protect me but also you enlighten me. It is your love that can help me overcome every difficulty I encounter. I will love you forever!

图 7

作文润色任务完成后，笔者要求学生上台展示，并要求他们结合自己的经验，详细讲述是如何润色作文的，以及所运用的技巧。该过程有助于学生自我诊断，发现自己在写作中存在的问题，同时也培养了自主学习能力。

(三) 迁移创新，提升思维品质

思维是智力和能力的核心。智力品质指的是在智力活动特别是思维活动中表现出来的智力和能力，因此，思维品质也被称为思维的智力品质。英语学习活动观强调培养学生的思维品质，迁移创新则要求学生综合运用语言技能，培养多元思维，实现深度学习，并将能力转化为素养。

在本课中，笔者要求学生利用所学技巧，用两三句话表达对祖国母亲的爱意并献上祝福。

T: In the previous letter, we expressed our love and gratitude to our mother. Similarly, it is important for us to express our love and wishes to our homeland. As we all know, this year marks the 70th anniversary of the founding of the People's Republic of China. Just like the famous phrase from the movie, *My Country, My People*, China has undergone tremendous transformation in the past seven decades, raising the living standards of its people. Therefore, I would like to convey my love and wishes to our

motherland with the learned skilled.

学生产出：

S1：My love for my country is as deep as the roots in fertile soil，nurtured by its rich history and brilliant culture. My heart is full of the pride for the beauty of its landscapes and the unity of its people.

S2：Love for my motherland is simple，yet profound. It's the pride in its past，the faith in its future，and the resolve to stand by its side always.

这个任务呼应了导入部分的内容。整个课堂的焦点从国家到家庭再到国家进行转换，突出了“家国情怀”的主题。通过这个任务的设置，笔者将语言能力的运用、学习能力的提升、思维品质的发展和文化意识的培养融为一体，帮助学生积极探索主题意义，发展思维，提升英语学科核心素养。

四、反思与总结

总的来说，本节写作课基本达到了既定的教学目标。笔者结合学生在课堂上的表现和教研员及其他学校教师的反馈，运用英语学习活动观对教学进行了反思。

首先，教师依托“家国情怀”的主题意义，落实了英语学科素养的培养。通过读、译、改、评等活动，将核心素养的目标融入学习理解、应用实践和迁移创新活动，体现了英语学习活动的综合性、关联性和实践性。其次，教师采用了自主合作的学习模式，促进学生进行深度学习。学生在小组合作中互相评价和竞争，积极参与到润色作文的任务中，发挥了主观能动性，提升了逻辑思维能力。

总之，在今后的教学中，教师要重视英语写作教学，积极探索并实践英语学习活动观，让学生运用所学的技巧和方法，创作出自己的作品，体验学习英语的乐趣，从而促进自身英语学科核心素养的有效形成，以此为落实立德树人根本任务打下基础。

参考文献

[1] 陈思琪.英语学习活动观下高中英语写前策略的应用[J].现代交际，2019(17)：231－232.

[2] 程晓堂.基于主题意义探究的英语教学理念与实践[J].中小学外语教学(中学篇)，2018,41(10)：1－7.

[3] 程晓堂,赵思奇.英语学科核心素养的实质内涵[J].课程·教材·教法，2016,36(05)：79－86.

[4] 卢银崧.在高中英语写作教学中落实英语学习活动观的实践[J].英语教师，2019,19(14)：121－126.

[5] 中华人民共和国教育部.普通高中英语课程标准(2017 年版 2020 年修订)[S].北京：人民教育出版社,2020.

案例 2

探究小组合作学习在高中英语写作教学中的应用

——以利弊类作文“The advantages and disadvantages of keeping a pet”为例

【摘　要】 课程标准强调了核心素养下的英语学习活动观以及自主学习、合作学习、探究学习等学习方式的重要性。传统的英语写作教学中存在教师主导、学生被动、评价单一等问题,这严重影响了学生的写作兴趣和效果。本研究将通过小组合作学习,以“养宠物的利与弊”为写作话题,开展高中英语写作教学。研究发现,小组合作学习能够促进学生之间的互动交流,提高学生的参与度,从而能有效提升学生的英语写作能力。这一研究有助于培养学生的英语学科核心素养,同时也为高中英语教师提供了新的教学思路和方法。

【关键词】 小组合作学习;高中英语写作;英语学科核心素养;利弊类作文

《普通高中英语课程标准(2017 年版 2020 年修订)》(本文以下简称“课程标准”)倡导指向学科核心素养的英语学习活动观和自主学习、合作学习、探究学习等学习方式。高中英语写作技能是英语学科知识技能的重要组成部分,但当前的高中英语教学中仍普遍采用“以教师讲解为主—学生被动接收—教师批改—范文呈现—学生背诵”的传统模式,从而导致学生的写作兴趣不高、写作内容贫乏,教师的评价单一、教学效果差等问题。在核心素养视域下,要想提高学生的英语写作能力,教师就需要改变传统的教学方式,把课堂的主体

地位还给学生。接下来,本文将对小组合作学习在高中英语写作教学中的应用进行探究。

一、合作学习的内涵

1. 课程标准的要求

课程标准提倡教师要引导学生采用自主、合作的学习方式,参与主题意义的探究活动,并学习语言知识,发展语言技能。教师在英语写作教学时要注意培养学生构思写作结构、列提纲、修改文章等的技能,这些写作技能都能够在合作学习中得到体现和培养。合作学习时,学生针对话题集思广益,列出提纲,运用自评、互评以及组内融合、组间竞争等多种形式进行写作,这对学生写作水平的提高及自主学习能力的培养有很大的促进作用。

2. 合作学习

美国学者罗伯特·斯莱文(Robert E. Slavin)指出,合作学习是指学生在小组中从事学习活动,以整个小组为单位,获得奖励或认可的课堂教学技术。王静展开了合作模式下英语写作策略习得的研究,明确指出合作学习能提升学生写作策略、构思能力和写作技巧,提升思维能力和交流能力。吴荣辉和何高大通过研究发现,合作学习对缓解学生的写作焦虑有很大帮助,学生对合作学习持积极态度。

我国学者曾琦整合出了合作学习的五大原则:(1) 正相互依赖,即每位组员为一个整体,紧密相关。(2) 个人责任,即每位组员在合作时要承担小组的对应职责。(3) 社交技能,在合作学习过程中,教师要让学生认识到运用社交技能的重要性,以确保合作学习在课堂中高效落实。(4) 小组自评,即每个小组要定期找出自己小组的不足及亮点,不断修正,从而提高合作效率。(5) 混合编组(3~5人),即分组时要根据学生的学习能力、性别、兴趣爱好等情况,发挥好个人特长,从而保证合作学习的高效性。

综上所述,合作学习是小组成员基于共同目标,通过相互沟通、相互鼓励,从而取得一定成果的学习活动。英语写作教学中的合作学习需要通过生生互动、师生互动,以促进合作学习任务的完成。在合作学习过程中,学生是主角,教师则是整个过程的引导者、协调者和组织者。

二、高中英语写作教学中合作学习的教学设计

1. 合理选材

教师在进行作文选题时，应尽量选择贴近学生生活、符合学生经验水平的作文题材，如“The advantages and disadvantages of keeping pets”“Living on campus or living at home, which do you prefer? Why?”等。这样才能更好地激发学生的写作兴趣，让学生有话可说。

2. 明确任务

教师要让每位组员明晰小组的共同任务和个人在组内的任务，为合作学习的展开奠定基础。如小组任务为“每个小组需提交一篇完整的文章”，组内任务为“每位成员需参与完成其中的一段”。

3. 教学环节

做好准备工作以后，教师便可开展写作活动了，主要包括写前、写作、评价与修改、点评与展示、激励这五个阶段。见表1。

表1　写作活动的五个阶段

写作阶段	操作过程	教学目标
1. 写前	教师导入话题，选择的话题为“Do you like keeping pets?”。教师可让学生进行头脑风暴，学生各抒己见。 每个小组讨论并列出饲养宠物的优缺点，分别至少3条，并列出相应的理由。随后，教师请小组代表汇报本小组的讨论结果。 学生独立列出初步的写作提纲(以思维导图形式呈现)。	教师通过贴近生活的“饲养宠物”的话题，成功地激起了学生的兴趣。在讨论中，学生进行了语言输出和输入，挖掘出了作文内容、结构、语言等方面的信息和要点，激活了写作思维。以上这些帮助学生搭建了写作支架，为下一步写作做好了铺垫。 学生通过小组讨论，集思广益，避免了陷入无话可讲的困境，从而缓解了写作焦虑。
2. 写作	学生进行独立写作，不能抄袭其他组员的写作内容。	组员根据本组讨论的内容及他组的汇报，将这些语言输出与自己掌握的信息转化为自己的写作内容。 在将来的学习和生活中，写作是一个独立思考的过程，因此非常有必要培养学生独立思考、独立写作的良好习惯。

续 表

写作阶段	操 作 过 程	教 学 目 标
3. 评价与修改	教师提供作文评价量表(附表 1),学生先自评。内容包括:写作内容是否切题,结构是否清晰,语言是否多样化,语法、拼写是否正确,等等。 学生修改完自己的习作后,可以进行小组互评。具体方法:将每个小组的学生进行编号,编号为 1、2 的学生互评,编号为 3、4 的学生互评。互评时不仅仅是简单地打分,更需要指出作文的优缺点。在需要改善的地方,需指出如何修改,不可泛泛而谈,并给予 3～5 句的评价。然后编号为 1、3 和 2、4 的学生再分别进行互评,要求同上。 各组长组织小组合作学习,并总结表现情况,完成合作反思。根据各组员的综合表现进行打分。(附表 2)	学生通过将自己的作文与评价量表的标准进行比较,发现自己的不足之处,从而主动改进,提升写作技能以及自主学习的能力。 学生之间的互评讨论有助于学生共同发现问题,拓展思维,获得更多的灵感与启发,同时也能缓解学生的写作焦虑。 学生通过及时总结合作学习中的问题,从而提高合作学习的效率。
4. 点评与展示	教师可选取个别学生的优秀习作进行点评。 教师也可选以小组为单位递交的"融合优秀作文"(即每位组员完成一段,并评价、修改其他组员的段落)进行点评。	学生通过阅读他人的作品,扬长避短、拓宽视野。 小组通过在全班展示"融合优秀作文",能够增强组内凝聚力,提高合作学习的效率。
5. 激励	对于优秀个人或团体进行多种形式的激励。如口头表扬,在教室里设置展示园地,给个人加分或评出优秀小组,给予小小的物质奖励,等等。	奖励或认可小组,是合作学习的重要策略和方法,能提升小组的凝聚力、激发学生学习的热情。

三、高中英语写作教学中合作学习的教学成效

通过一段时间的合作学习,学生的写作水平明显提高,具体表现为:

(1) 学生通过合作学习拓宽了视野,能更合理地处理文章结构、厘清文章思路、使用过渡词和主题句,文章的词汇、句型也变得更加多样化,写作能力明显提高。

(2) 学生通过合作学习缓解了写作焦虑,增强了写作信心。合作学习小组中分布着学习水平不同的学生,他们可以相互沟通并借鉴组内成员的成功经验;同时,当学生在组内受到他人的鼓励与赞扬时,其写作信心也会增强;再次,当以

小组为单位递交的作文被教师表扬并得到鼓励时，学生的集体荣誉感和学习热情会被激发。

(3) 学生的写作成绩有了一定程度的提高。

四、高中英语写作教学中合作学习的意义

1. 转变教师教学理念

“问渠那得清如许？为有源头活水来。”教师的力量来自教师不断转变自身的教学理念，更新自身的专业知识。时代在飞速地发展，教学理念也须与时俱进。“满堂灌”的教学理念和方法显然已经无法满足当今世界对学生素养和技能的要求。教师必须从源头即教学理念上发生转变，把课堂的主体地位还给学生，采用形式丰富的课堂活动进行教学，以达到提升学生的核心素养和技能的目标。

2. 发展学生核心素养

传统的写作教学模式造成了种种问题，但相比之下，在合作教学中，学生通过分组进行组内沟通、学生自评、生生互评以及师生互评等，缓解了学生的写作焦虑，提升了写作的自信。小组的合作和竞争关系，最终促成了学生语言能力、学习能力、思维品质、文化意识等核心素养的融合发展，使得学生的学习更具自主性。

五、结语

综上所述，将合作学习应用于高中英语写作是一种有效的教学方式。当然，英语写作并不仅限于一种教学方式，针对不同文体、不同选材、不同学生，可以采用不同的教学方式。新时代的教师，应该勇于尝试不同的教学方法和形式，使学生进行深入知识内核的学习，聚焦学生学科核心素养的培养、践行课堂教学以学生为主体的理念，从而推动课堂教学的转型。

参考文献

[1] 程晓堂.核心素养下的英语教学理论与实践[M].南宁：广西教育出版社，2021.

[2] 王静.合作学习模式下学习者英语写作策略习得研究[J].继续教育研究，2010(04)：157－159.

[3] 吴荣辉，何高大.合作学习在大学英语写作教学中的应用效应研究[J].外语

教学，2014,35(03)：44－47.

[4] 曾琦.合作学习的基本要素[J].学科教育，2000(06)：7－12.

[5] 中华人民共和国教育部.普通高中英语课程标准(2017年版2020年修订)[S].北京：人民教育出版社,2020.

[6] 钟嫵.合作学习对提升高中英语写作能力的作用[D].上海：华东师范大学,2017.

[7] Slavin R. E. Cooperative learning[J]. Review of Educational Research, 1980,50(02)：315－342.

附表1

学生作文评价量表(自评/互评)

<table>
<tr><td></td><td>标准描述</td><td colspan="5">得分</td></tr>
<tr><td rowspan="6">内容
(10分)</td><td></td><td colspan="2">三档
(4分)</td><td colspan="2">二档
(2分)</td><td>一档
(0分)</td></tr>
<tr><td>1. 审题准确。</td><td colspan="2"></td><td colspan="2"></td><td></td></tr>
<tr><td></td><td>五档
(2分)</td><td>四档
(1.5分)</td><td>三档
(1分)</td><td>二档
(0.5分)</td><td>一档
(0分)</td></tr>
<tr><td>2. 要点齐全,满足题目要求。</td><td></td><td></td><td></td><td></td><td></td></tr>
<tr><td>3. 聚焦主题且有翔实的支撑性材料/细节。</td><td></td><td></td><td></td><td></td><td></td></tr>
<tr><td>4. 层次详略得当。</td><td></td><td></td><td></td><td></td><td></td></tr>
<tr><td rowspan="5">语言
(10分)</td><td>1. 句型变化多样且得体有效。</td><td></td><td></td><td></td><td></td><td></td></tr>
<tr><td>2. 用词丰富得当,有一定的超纲词汇。</td><td></td><td></td><td></td><td></td><td></td></tr>
<tr><td>3. 语法结构正确,只有少数语法错误。</td><td></td><td></td><td></td><td></td><td></td></tr>
<tr><td>4. 运用了恰当的衔接手法,行文流畅,有自己的语言风格。</td><td></td><td></td><td></td><td></td><td></td></tr>
<tr><td>5. 没有拼写、标点和大小写错误。</td><td></td><td></td><td></td><td></td><td></td></tr>
</table>

续　表

	标　准　描　述	得　　分		
		三档(1分)	二档(0.5分)	一档(0分)
结构 (5分)	1. 有恰当的开头、中间和结尾。			
	2. 分段合理且有清晰的主题句和过渡句。			
	3. 段落之间和段落内部整体连贯,逻辑合理。			
	4. 体现文体(如记叙文、议论文、应用文等)。			
	5. 卷面整洁。			
总分:				
习作亮点 2～5句评价				
修改建议				

附表 2

小组合作学习表

小组:							
组员	对小组的贡献(内容、词汇、句型结构等)	1. 明确个人任务	2. 参与讨论	3. 认真倾听	4. 帮助他人	5. 虚心请教	6. 按时完成作业
备注:							
小组合作学习反思 1. 此次活动,我们小组做得比较好的两个方面是: 2. 此次活动,我们小组做得不足的两个方面是哪两个?该如何改进?							

注:1～6项每项5分,共30分。

案例3

思维导图在高中英语写作教学中的应用

——以黄浦区2023届高三一模作文题为例

【摘　要】 课程标准要求学生提升写作能力以进行有效的沟通，但许多高中生的表达能力较弱，教师的教学方法也有待优化。思维导图是一种有效的图形工具，能归纳信息、激发思维潜能。本研究通过一个建议信的写作教学案例，在多个教学环节中引入思维导图，探讨其在提高高中生英语写作能力中的适用性和有效性，以期为学生和教师提供新的学习和教学思路。

【关键词】 高中英语写作；建议信写作；思维导图

一、引言

根据《普通高中英语课程标准(2017年版2020年修订)》，学生需要整合语言知识，有效使用书面语等语言形式，得体且恰当地与他人沟通和交流。许多高中生在写作方面的能力还比较薄弱，无法恰当地表达观点，常出现词不达意等情况。加上部分教师缺少有效的写作教学方式，导致课堂乏味，进一步降低了学生对写作的兴趣。因此，教师需要寻求新的教学方法以提高学生的写作能力。

思维导图是表达放射性思维的图形工具，可用于归纳信息和挖掘思维潜能。将思维导图用于高中英语写作教学，可激发学生的思维，帮助其梳理文章逻辑，提高其写作兴趣。本文将基于思维导图，进行英语写作课的教学设计，探究其在高中英语写作教学中的适用性和有效性。

二、思维导图

1. 思维导图的概念

20世纪六七十年代，英国心理学家东尼·博赞(Tony Buzan)发明了思维导图，他在其著作中正式提出了这个概念，并将其与“记笔记”和“做笔记”相对应。“记笔记”是记录和整理别人的思想，而“做笔记”是激发和整理自己的思想。国内著名教育学者赵国庆分析得出，思维导图的核心目的是激发和整理思考，它采用非线性的笔记方式，从中心向周围发散。其将思维导图定义为促进思维激发和思维整理的可视化、非线性思维工具。

2. 思维导图的特点

思维导图具有多方位、系统性和个性化等特点。它不仅是放射性思维的表达方式，也是开启大脑潜力的通用工具。放射性思维是一种扩散性与求异性并存的思维模式，旨在从多个角度和层面来探索问题，通过拓宽视野、激发思维来突破认知局限，并产生独特的新见解。

思维导图始终围绕一个关键词或主题展开，使用者可以从不同角度对其进行分析。通过多彩的线条将几千个节点相互连接，水平的节点之间具有横向关联、上下的节点之间具有纵向关联；同时每个节点都可以成为新的中心，并继续向外延伸，最终形成一个逻辑清晰、层次分明的系统。

思维导图的个性化特征有利于不同使用者绘制出符合其个性的思维导图。正是因为这种独特的信息差，使得思维导图更具创造性和趣味性，能够激发使用者的创造力和积极性。

3. 思维导图在英语写作教学中的运用

思维导图在中国的流行始于 2005 年东尼·博赞在中国进行的一系列推广活动。自此，国内各学科教师开始在实践中运用思维导图，探索其辅助教学的功能。在高中英语教学中，教育研究者们通过综述、案例分析和实验研究等方式，探讨了思维导图在高中英语写作教学中的适用性和有效性。但是，到目前为止，这些研究大多以文字形式呈现，缺乏可视化的表达方式。此外，相关研究主要集中在写前环节或某个话题的思维导图构建，缺乏将思维导图应用于整堂写作课的教学设计研究。

三、思维导图在高中英语写作教学中的实践案例

本研究以黄浦区 2023 届高三一模的作文题为基础，以可视化的方式将思维导图运用于写前、写中和写后的各个环节，以探究思维导图在高中英语写作教学中的适用性和有效性。

1. 教学内容分析

本节课是高三第一学期的一节作文课，选用的教学内容是黄浦区 2023 届高三一模的作文题。

> 假设你是明启中学学生李华，学校正在征求学生对云课堂的感受和建议。请发送一封邮件至校长信箱，你的邮件内容须包括：
>
> 1. 详细描述一节云课堂以及你的感受；
>
> 2. 简单阐述你对云课堂的态度和建议。

本节课属于建议信教学的第三课时。在前两个课时，教师已对建议信的基本框架结构和语言特点做了介绍，给学生布置了一篇习作，并进行了批改、分析和点评，发现学生习作中存在不少问题。所以这节课属于复习课，教学重点是要夯实学生对建议信基本框架结构的掌握及解决学生习作中存在的一些问题，以达到让学生熟练掌握写作建议信的目的。

2. 学情分析

该节课的教学对象为高三第一学期的学生，他们的学习能力属于年级中等水平，思维较为活跃，乐于进行小组合作。他们已上过两个课时的建议信方面的内容，基本了解了建议信的框架结构、语言特点等内容。但是通过之前的练习、学生访谈和学生问卷，反映出一些问题：部分学生对于建议信审题不够仔细和准确，不能清晰把握写信人和收信人之间的关系；部分学生对于建议信的首、尾段处理过于复杂，所占篇幅过重；学生对于建议信的语言掌握不够熟练，导致无话可说；等等。基于这些问题，教师旨在通过思维导图，帮助学生在写作结构、写作内容和写作语言上搭建支架，提升学生写作建议信的水平。

3. 教学目标

① 学会分析作者与目标读者之间的关系。(To learn to analyze the relationship between the writer and the target reader.)

② 巩固建议信的基本结构。(To consolidate the basic structure of an advice letter.)

③ 让学生熟悉建议信中使用的语言。(To familiarize the students with the language used in the advice letter.)

④ 学会使用恰当的语言，尤其是在文章的尾段。(To learn to use the proper language, especially in the last paragraph.)

⑤ 学会运用思维导图厘清思路。(To learn to use the mind map to clarify the ideas.)

4. 教学设计

（1）导入：创设情境，明确写作目的

学生应该被告知写作的真正目的，知道他们“为什么”写作，以及他们“为谁”写作。王蔷曾提到，当学生有真实的写作目的、写作对象时，会有更强烈的写作意愿。

导入环节的一大重要作用就是创设真实的情境，让学生在真实的情境中运用语言。在本节课中，教师首先向学生展示了一组疫情期间的照片，以期唤起学生真实的回忆，然后教师提问：“Do you like studying online?”学生七嘴八舌，共同回忆那段上网课的岁月。在与学生的互动中，教师相机引入写作任务——描述一节网课以及对网课的态度与建议。

（2）写前活动：激活图式、构建框架、助力写作

王德美在其研究中指出，一半以上的学生写作时不知如何对存储在记忆中的语言知识进行调取和使用，且大部分学生不能用英语表达自己的想法。这表明学生写作的主要困难仍在知识的调取和使用以及语言表达等方面。

为了帮助学生克服写作困难，可以采用基于思维导图的写前活动。思维导图运用在写前阶段有几个好处。首先，能激发学生的思维，帮助他们产生丰富的观点，并以清晰有序的方式展现出来。其次，思维导图可以帮助学生整理语篇的框架结构，加强对文本的理解。最后，思维导图有助于学生调动和运用已有的语言知识，使其转化为语言技能，从而促进综合运用能力的提高。这一阶段的设计要有的放矢，分步骤进行，为学生的写中活动做好准备。据此，可以设计下述两个任务：

① 头脑风暴，激活遗忘的图式

本节课为建议信的第三课时，学生对于建议信的基本框架结构已经有了了解，但是部分学生在图式方面有所遗忘。可以通过全班头脑风暴的形式，激活学生遗忘的结构图式，并由教师在黑板上同步呈现以下结构图式，如图1所示。

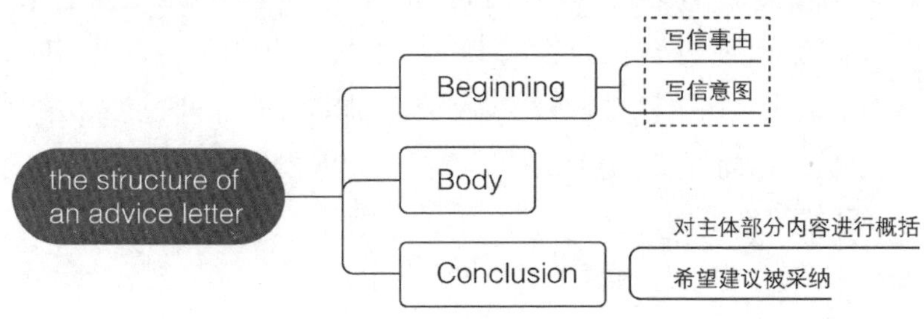

图1　建议信的基本框架结构

接下来，再次通过全班头脑风暴，在已有的思维导图的基础上，进一步提取学生已有的相关语言，如图 2 所示。

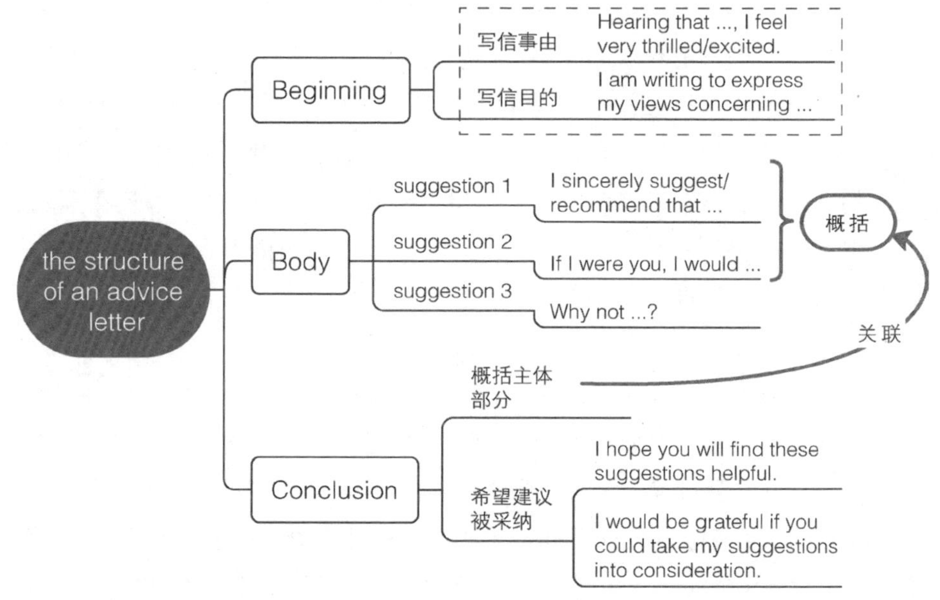

图 2　建议信常用句型

② 发散思维，构建信件主体

在头脑风暴后，学生以小组为单位进行合作学习，一起探讨、建构信件的主体部分。对主体部分的结构，有哪些处理建议并说明理由是本次写作的重点，也是学生写作过程中的难点。通过思维导图所呈现的主体部分结构清晰、逻辑连贯，不仅能激发学生产生新的观点，还能帮助学生梳理内容和结构，为学生提供充足的支架，助力学生完成写作任务。信件要求学生详细描述一节云课堂，以及阐述对云课堂的态度、感受和建议。因此主体部分结构可以用图 3 呈现。

这里选取的是某个小组的合作成果。当然，每个小组都有自己不同的方案，教师可以让小组代表在全班进行分享、展示，再加以点评。通过思维导图发散思维，学生对于建议信的框架、句型结构、写作内容以及建议理由等已了然于心，接下来就可以开始写作了。

(3) 写中活动：借助思维导图，完成写作任务

经过一系列的写前活动，学生已经明确了本次的写作目标、写信对象和写作

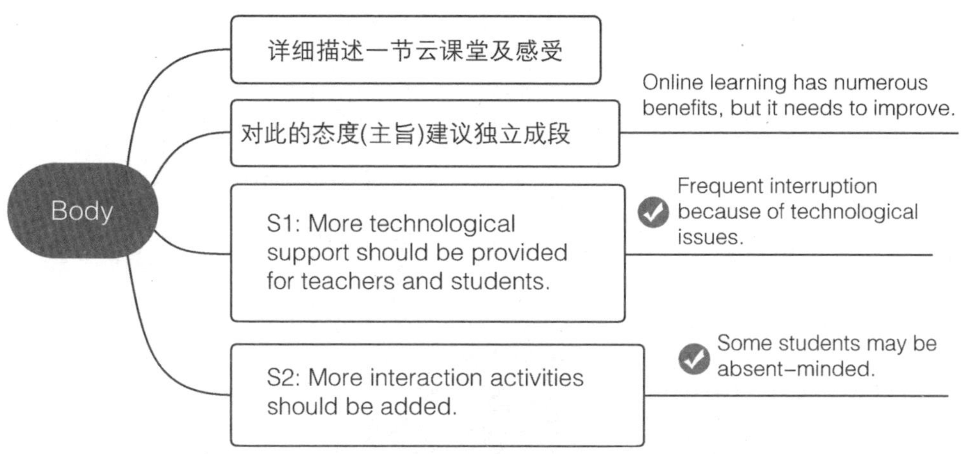

图 3　主体部分的框架结构(某个小组的合作成果)

内容,他们的写作热情也被充分激发起来。除此之外,学生通过思维导图的构建,掌握了相关语料,建立了写作框架,并初步形成了自己的建议信。在写中这个阶段,教师需要明确写作的具体要求,鼓励学生以思维导图为基础完成写作任务,并实现个性化的表达;同时,提醒学生在写作过程中应注意细节,比如时态的使用、信件格式、单词拼写和书写规范等;教师还需提醒学生注意写信对象为校长,因此措辞上应更婉转才比较妥当。

(4) 写后活动:制定评价标准,进行自评、互评

评价反馈在学生写作中是非常重要的一环。教师引导学生使用基于思维导图的评价标准进行自我评价和互相评价,能够帮助写作者修改文章以及提高文章质量。相较于传统的评价标准,思维导图构建的评价标准更加丰富多彩,条理更加清晰,重点更加突出。它能够激发学生的视觉神经,使得学生能够迅速捕捉到重点,从而进行更加高效的评价,如图 4 所示。

四、结语

将思维导图运用于高中英语写作教学中,可以帮助学生厘清文章的行文逻辑,丰富他们的词汇表达,并能有效地评价他们的写作成果。学生有效地运用书面语表达观点并进行人际交流的能力得到了提升,有助于学生语言综合运用能力的提高,因此思维导图是提高学生写作能力的有效方式。

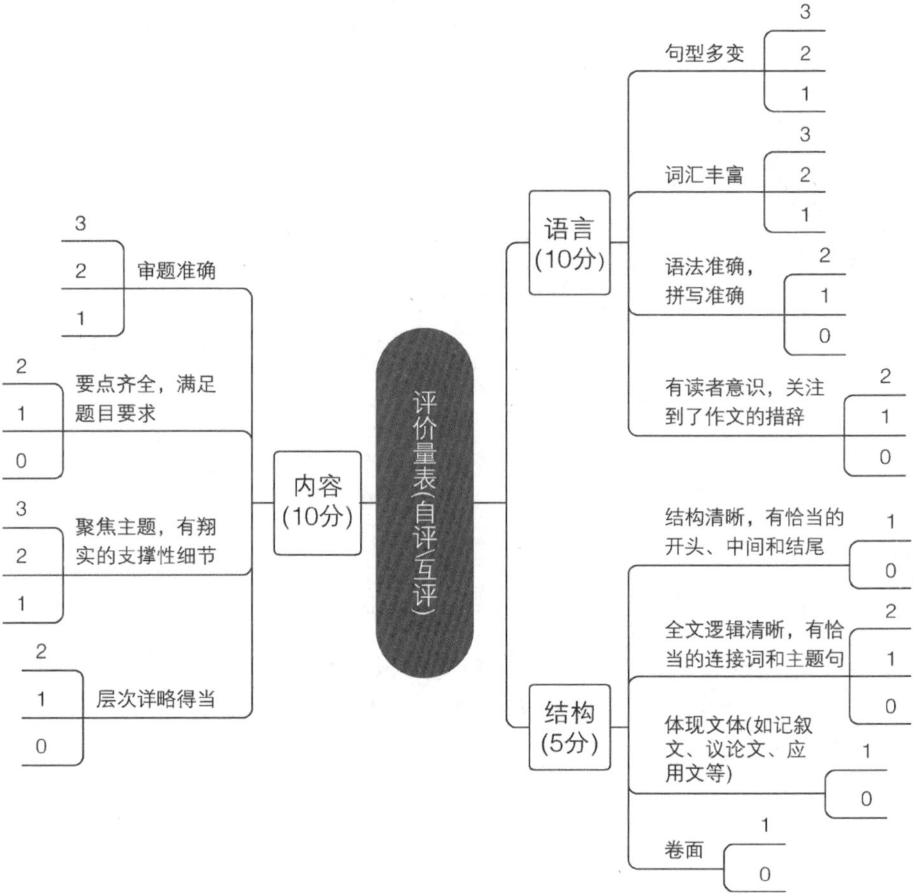

- 评价量表(自评/互评)
  - 内容(10分)
    - 审题准确：3 / 2 / 1
    - 要点齐全，满足题目要求：2 / 1 / 0
    - 聚焦主题，有翔实的支撑性细节：3 / 2 / 1
    - 层次详略得当：2 / 1 / 0
  - 语言(10分)
    - 句型多变：3 / 2 / 1
    - 词汇丰富：3 / 2 / 1
    - 语法准确，拼写准确：2 / 1 / 0
    - 有读者意识，关注到了作文的措辞：2 / 1 / 0
  - 结构(5分)
    - 结构清晰，有恰当的开头、中间和结尾：1 / 0
    - 全文逻辑清晰，有恰当的连接词和主题句：2 / 1 / 0
    - 体现文体(如记叙文、议论文、应用文等)：1 / 0
    - 卷面：1 / 0

图 4　思维导图形式的评价量表

参考文献

[1] 陈丹丹.动态评价视角下网络同伴互评对英语写作质量的影响[J].外语电化教学,2021(02)：17－23,3.

[2] 李玥瑶.思维导图在高中英语写作教学中的应用[J].教育教学论坛，2013(50)：226－227.

[3] 任永东,张健.论过程体裁法在高中英语写作教学中的应用[J].中国教育学刊，2014(05)：80－83.

[4] 托尼·巴赞.思维导图——放射性思维[M].李斯,译.北京：世界图书出版

公司北京公司，2004.
[5] 王德美.高中生英语写作现状调查与策略探讨[J].基础教育课程，2019(10)：43-48.
[6] 王蔷.英语教学法教程[M].2版.北京：高等教育出版社，2006.
[7] 许幸，刘玉梅.多模态理论视域下英语写作写前动机培养的实证研究[J].外语电化教学，2018(01)：25-31.
[8] 赵国庆.概念图、思维导图教学应用若干重要问题的探讨[J].电化教育研究，2012，33(05)：78-84.
[9] 中华人民共和国教育部.普通高中英语课程标准(2017年版2020年修订)[S].北京：人民教育出版社，2020.
[10] Buzan T. The Buzan study skills handbook[M]. London: BBC ACTIVE, 2006.

附学生习作

Dear Headmaster,

Hearing our school is collecting ideas and suggestions on the online class, as a student at Mingqi High School, I would like to share my thoughts and feedback on the online classroom experience.

First of all, I would like to describe my experience in a recent online class. 【主题句】The teacher utilized/used various multimedia tools and interactive platforms to deliver the lesson content effectively. The virtual classroom created an engaging atmosphere, allowing students to participate actively through real-time discussions and polls. The seamless integration of audio and video functionalities made the learning experience dynamic and immersive.

Regarding my attitude towards online classrooms, I believe they have numerous advantages. Firstly, they offer flexibility, allowing students to access course materials and lectures at their convenience. Secondly, virtual classrooms provide opportunities for students to develop self-discipline and time management skills. Additionally, online platforms enable teachers to incorporate multimedia resources, such as videos, interactive exercises, and e-books, which can enhance the learning experience.

However, I do have a few suggestions for improvement. Firstly, it would be beneficial to provide clear guidelines and instructions for both students and teachers to ensure smooth navigation through the virtual classroom. Secondly, continuous technical support and troubleshooting assistance should be available to address any potential issues that may arise during online classes. Lastly, incorporating more collaborative activities and group projects within the virtual classroom could enhance student interaction and foster teamwork.

Thank you for considering my feedback. I would appreciate it very much if you could take my suggestions into consideration.

Yours sincerely,

Li Hua

案例 4

高中英语写作教学教、学、评一体化的实践探索

【摘　要】 本文讨论了高中英语写作教学中教、学、评一体化的实践探索。教学评价在提升教学质量方面起到了关键作用。课程标准提出了教、学、评一体化的理念,将评价融入教学过程。这一新模式打破了教学和评价二元分离的局面,使教学活动与评价紧密相连。本研究通过一节高二的英语写作课,将教、学、评一体化的理念贯彻实施在课堂的各个教学环节中,旨在提高教师的写作教学效率以及学生的写作能力。

【关键词】 高中英语写作;教学评价;教、学、评一体化

一、引言

教学评价是检测教学目标落实成效的有效手段之一,对提升教学质量能起到关键作用。《普通高中英语课程标准(2017 年版 2020 年修订)》提出教师应处理好评价与教和学之间的关系,推动教、学、评一体化实施。该理念备受理论研究者和实践者的关注。这种教、学、评一体化的新模式将评价嵌入教学过程,打破了传统教学和评价的二元分离。新模式使得教学活动

与评价紧密相连，使评价的关注重点从学习结果转移到学习过程。这一模式的出现，促使英语教学在整体规划方面更注重“教什么”“怎样教”和“教得如何”等。针对高中英语课堂中的重要内容——英语写作，从写作教学、学习和评价三要素进行系统设计和实施研究，有助于以过程性的方式推进“以评促教”和“以评促学”，并探索高中英语写作教学中教、学、评一体化的实践经验。

二、教、学、评一体化的理念及整体设计

教、学、评指的是一个完整教学活动的三个方面，一体化则指这三个方面的统一融合。《普通高中英语课程标准(2017 年版 2020 年修订)》指出：“完整的教学活动包括教、学、评三个方面。‘教’是教师把握英语学科核心素养的培养方向，通过有效组织和实施课内外教与学的活动，达成学科育人的目标；‘学’是学生在教师的指导下，通过主动参与各种语言实践活动，将学科知识和技能转化为自身的学科核心素养；‘评’是教师依据教学目标确定评价内容和评价标准，通过组织和引导学生完成以评价目标为导向的多种评价活动，以此监控学生的学习过程，检测教与学的效果，实现以评促学，以评促教。”王蔷、李亮的“教、学、评一体化设计与实施的相关要素分析”见图 1。

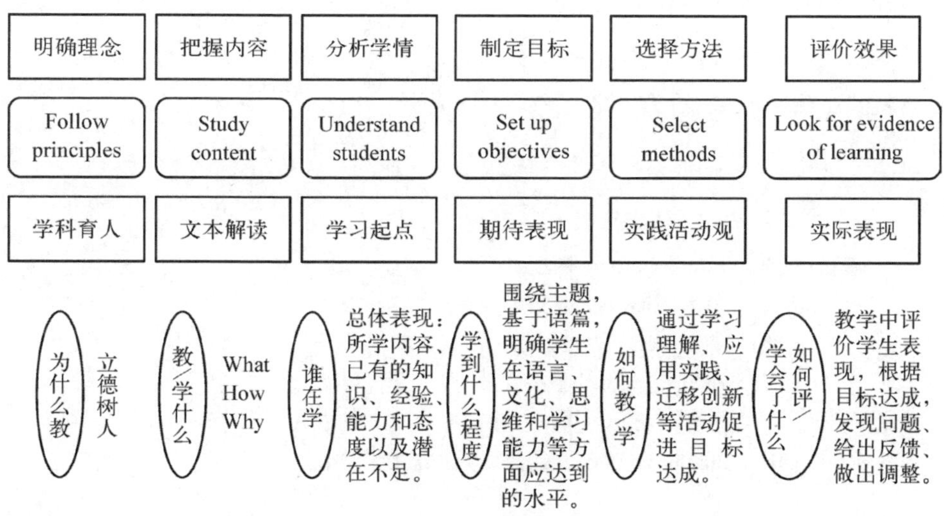

图 1　教、学、评一体化设计与实施的相关要素分析

教、学、评一体化课程的融合设计可以分为"课前""课中""课后"三个阶段。

(1) 课前阶段：在明确立德树人理念、发展学科核心素养的前提下，教师需明确教学目标，即"教什么""怎么教"和"为什么教"，而学生需要清楚"学什么"。教师可以通过安置性评价获取信息和相关数据，了解学情，从而制定教学目标。整节课的设计应该以教学目标为导向。

(2) 课中阶段：在制定完教学目标后，教师应选择合理的教学方法，通过一系列课堂活动来达成教学目标。教师应根据不同的课堂活动制定评价内容和评价策略，以形成性评价的方式引领学生进行反思，巩固学习所得和调整学习策略，最终达成学习目标。

(3) 课后阶段：教师可以根据所教内容进行评价，如作业评价或阶段性测评等。这些评价也可以作为后续教学内容的安置性评价。

三、高中英语写作教学教、学、评一体化的案例设计与分析

基于上述教、学、评一体化的设计理念，我们以高二第一学期的一节英语写作教学课为例，开展英语写作教学案例设计与分析。

(一) 教学内容分析

以下为本节课的写作要求：

你是明启中学高二学生李华。学校新建了一个图书馆，有下列类别的图书。请给某学生杂志投稿，介绍你们学校的图书馆，并说明你最喜欢的是哪一类图书。(见图 2)

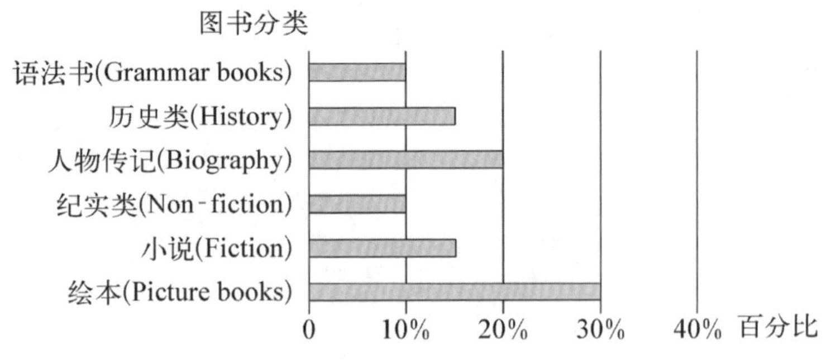

图 2　学生喜欢的图书分析图

这是一节作文课，重难点是要教会学生如何审题、如何写好一个段落，特别是如何写好一个主题句。

（二）学情分析

本节课的教学对象为高二第一学期某市重点学校平行班的学生，他们从高二才开始接触英语写作，对高中英语的写作技巧、写作策略等掌握得不够熟练。

教师在课前进行了安置性评价，如学生访谈、学生问卷和作业评价等，发现学生在写作方面存在以下主要问题：

(1) 审题不清。不少学生在审题时不清楚写信人的身份，也不清楚读信人是谁，缺少作者意识和读者意识。

(2) 不会写主题句。不少学生不清楚什么样的句子才是一个好的主题句。

(3) 不会展开段落。部分学生在展开段落时没有支撑性细节或者不清楚展开的策略，因此经常会出现无话可说的问题。

根据安置性评价的结果，教师制定了本节课的教学目标。

（三）教学目标

(1) 了解作者与目标读者之间的关系。(To learn the relationship between the writer and the target reader.)

(2) 知道一个好的主题句的基本结构。(To know the basic structure of a good topic sentence.)

(3) 掌握显示支撑性细节的常用方法。(To command common methods of flashing out supporting details.)

(4) 完成整篇文章。(To write the whole passage.)

（四）教学活动

在写作学习活动中，以目标为导向，通过整合教学和评价任务，让学生进行一系列活动，包括构思结构框架、小组合作、实践写作以及评价修改等。在教学过程中，我们强调整合教学、学习和评价的设计，其中评价非常重要，而反馈是评价的核心，它能够提供有助于学习的重要信息。通过教师的指导，学生参与活动，并不断接受反馈和校正，调整学习策略，实现学习目标。下面是具体的写作活动安排：

1. 展示写作教学目标

教师在进行简洁明了的课堂导入后，就在 PPT 上展示本节课的教学目标。（见图 3）

LEARNING OBJECTIVES

(a) To learn the relationship between the writer and the target reader.

(b) To know the basic structure of a good topic sentence.

(c) To command common methods of flashing out supporting details.

(d) To write the whole passage.

图 3

通过教师展示的教学目标，学生在本节课一开始就知道要“学什么”，最终的目标指向是什么。

2. 培养写作目标意识

基于安置性评价中的学生反馈——审题时不够仔细，特别是在作者意识和读者意识上有所缺失，因此教师在展示题目要求时，在 PPT 上圈画了关键信息。（见图 4）

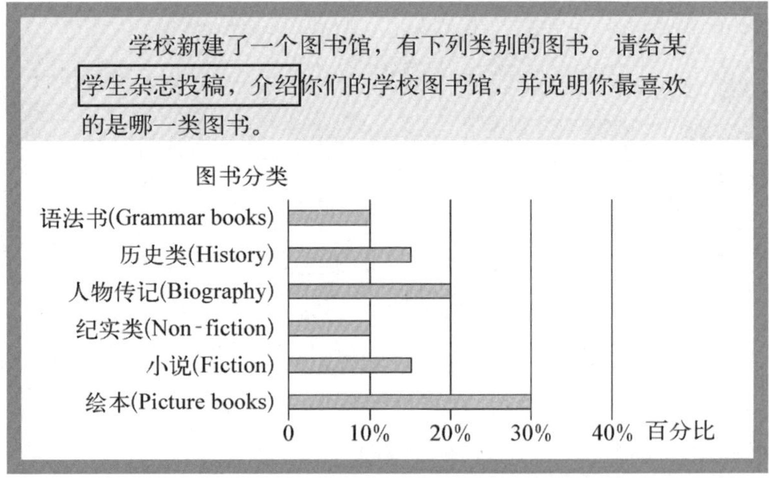

图 4

教师帮助学生明确作者角色为“某校学生”、目标读者为“杂志读者——学生”、体裁是“投稿——说明文”、议题性质是“书籍”、目的是“介绍校图书馆，并说明喜欢的书籍的类型及原因”。（见表 1）通过培养写作意识，学生学会了辨识“作者角色”“读者意识”“文体意识”“写作目的”等具体要素，强化了写作“元认知策略”。

表 1　写作意识

作者(Role)	读者(Audience)	体裁(Format)	议题(Topic)	目的(Purpose)
某校学生	杂志读者——学生	投稿——说明文	书籍	介绍校图书馆，并说明喜欢的书籍的类型及原因

3. 构思与修改写作框架

依据写作要求，学生讨论提炼写作要点并分析隐含信息，以思维导图的方式建构出写作结构并进行展示，以便教师进行口头反馈评价。（见图 5）

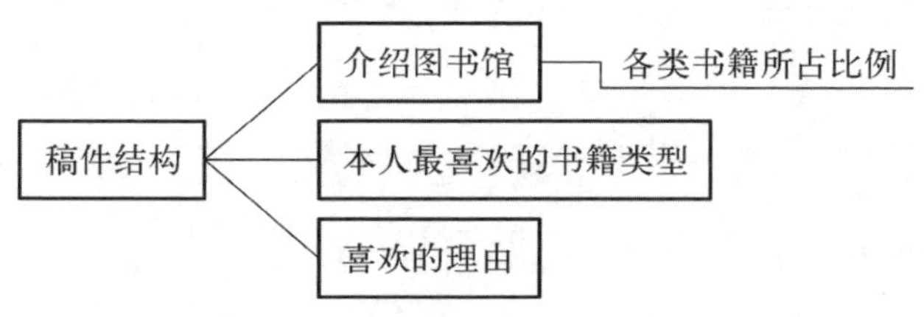

图 5　写作框架图(评价修改前)

教师通过观察发现，在建构要点时学生存在以下问题并对此进行即时反馈：

(1) 在介绍图书馆时，提醒学生既然是新建的图书馆，是否可以简单涉及图书馆的建立时间和具体位置等信息；

(2) 学生阐述喜欢的理由过于单一，提醒学生是否至少应写两个理由；

(3) 文章最后是否还需要加一个总结，使得文章更为完整；

(4) 整篇文章是否可以采用“五段式”的结构。

经过师生共评，学生对写作框架进行了修改。（见图 6）

在本节课的教学活动中，教师及时给予学生口头反馈评价，并引导他们进行思考，对自己的稿件结构进行调整和修改。教师的评价与反馈侧重给出确切、描述性的建议，以帮助学生进行自我诊断，并在写作前构建相对完整的写作要点。

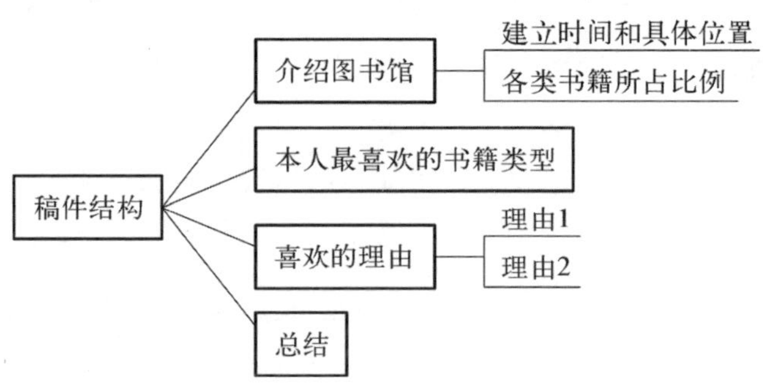

图 6　写作框架图示(评价修改后)

4. 搭建主题句支架与评价

尽管师生们在上一个教学活动中已经提炼出每段的核心主题,但根据所做的安置性评价,学生对于如何把每段的核心主题用一句恰当的主题句来表达仍然存在困难。因此,教师首先通过搭建主题句的支架,展示"主题句＝一个主题＋一个中心思想(topic sentence＝one topic＋one controlling idea)",让学生明晰何为一句好的主题句;然后带着学生一起判断 PPT 上的两句主题句的不足之处,并进行修改。(见图 7)

reasons for your choice

➢ topic sentence =one topic + one controlling idea

Grammar books

- ~~Books~~ can be a powerful tool to help me command English rules.
- Grammar books can help me deal with grammatical problems ~~and improve my academic performance.~~

图 7

随后,教师拆掉支架,让学生自己选择喜欢的书籍,写出理由段落的主题句,并上黑板展示。学生根据教师所给的评价标准(见图 8),评价反馈哪个主题句是最佳主题句。最后,教师再给予一定的点评。

Write a topic sentence for your choice.

self-assessment and peer-assessment

Checklist	Me	My partner 1	My partner 2
• one complete sentence			
• one clear topic			
• one focused controlling idea			

√=yes　　×=no　　?=not sure

图 8

在这个教、学、评一体化的教学活动中，学生对于主题句的理解和领悟从模糊到清晰，再到自己能写出主题句，最后到能够评价什么是好的主题句。教师和学生的评价在其中起到了非常重要的作用。教师通过及时反馈，帮助学生修正理解，从而让其掌握了知识和技能。

5. 构建段落与评价

单靠一句好的主题句无法构建一个好的段落。教师随即向学生展示 PPT。(见图 9)

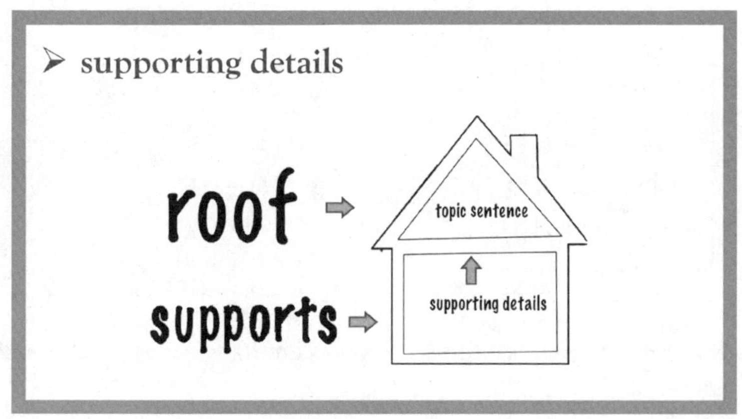

图 9

一个内容翔实的段落应包含"一个主题句＋一些支撑性细节(a topic

sentence＋supporting details)”，而这些支撑性细节需要用多样性的写作技巧呈现出来。教师通过 a、b、c、d 四个例子(受篇幅限制，此处不列出)呈现了四种重要的写作技巧：对比法、假设法、举例法、因果分析法。(见图 10)

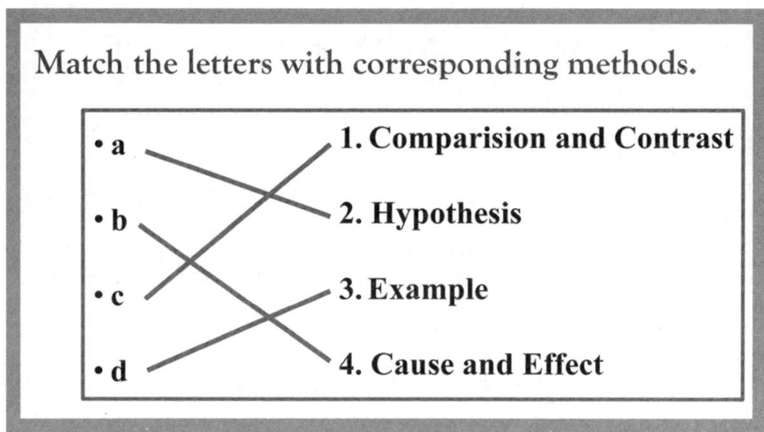

图 10

接下来，教师拆掉支架并呈现评价标准，让学生独立完成一个段落的写作，进行自评和互评。(见图 11)

self-assessment and peer-assessment

Checklist	Me	My partner
• logical and focused supporting details		
• correct method of flashing out details		

√=yes ×=no ?=not sure

图 11

在这个教、学、评一体化的环节中，教师教给学生段落的组成架构和写作技巧，学生不但学会了，并且在最后的评价部分，明晰了评价标准，并通过自评和互评对段落进行了调整和修正。

6. 课后独立写作及评价

课堂的讲解环节结束后，教师要求学生独立完成整篇文章的写作，并要求学生按照评价清单（见表 2）展开自评和互评，各自记录需要修改的要点并进行二次写作。学生完成修改后，教师可在第二节课提出"你认为第二次写作与第一次相比有什么改变?"的问题。由此，学生可以看到学习行为与学习成效之间的关联，有助于其增强写作信心并提升学习能力。

表2　评价清单

维　度	要　　点	评价与建议
篇章结构	文章结构是否完整	
	是否根据写作内容合理分段	
	是否在语句间使用了逻辑关联词使内容连贯	
文章内容	要点是否涵盖全面	
	是否添加了与内容相关的必要细节	
语言运用	动词使用是否恰当	
	时态是否正确	
	句子结构是否完整	
其他	文章篇幅是否符合要求	
	标点符号是否使用正确	
	书写是否清楚、工整	

由此可见，教师在教学中不仅要传递教学目标和协商评价标准，还需要及时判断和反馈学生的具体表现，收集学生的学习信息。学生在教师的指导下，通过参与小组讨论、全班协商、头脑风暴、独立写作、共同反思与评价等语言实践活动，将写作意识与知识转化为具体的写作策略和技能。教学中的评价将学生的行为与评价标准关联，将行为与策略关联，并对学生的表现给予具体、及时的反

馈，关注行为产生的效果。这一系列活动关注了写作教学中的“教什么”“学什么”“如何教”“如何学”“教得如何”以及“学得如何”，由此形成了教、学、评一体化的框架。

四、结语

教、学、评一体化是一种教学设计和实施的综合策略，既注重教学目标的设定，又关注评价任务和学习活动的设计。我们从教学目标出发，明确评价任务，并设计相应的学习活动。这种教学模式强调以目标为导向，将教和学相结合，并将评价贯穿全过程，形成一个动态循环。这样的教学过程不仅关注学生在每个关键阶段的学习效果，也为学习的发生创造了条件、为学习的发展提供了方向，真正达到“以评促教”和“以评促学”的效果。

参考文献

[1] 蒋京丽.以评促教促学，落实英语教、学、评一体化的五点实施建议[J].英语学习，2021(09)：4-9.

[2] 蒋银华.目标导向下“教—学—评一致性”的课堂设计[J].中小学管理，2013(01)：12-14.

[3] 卢臻.教—学—评一体化教学揭秘[J].基础教育课程，2016(07)：8-11,28.

[4] 王蔷，李亮.推动核心素养背景下英语课堂教—学—评一体化：意义、理论与方法[J].课程·教材·教法，2019,39(05)：114-120.

[5] 王少非.课堂评价[M].上海：华东师范大学出版社，2013.

[6] 吴星，吕琳.核心素养培养需要“教、学、评”一体化[J].江苏教育，2019(19)：22-25.

[7] 袁树厚.走进外语课堂教学的形成性评估之促学研究[J].外国语言文学，2017,34(04)：274-279.

[8] 张洁.智慧管理与调控——课堂教学有效的基本保障[J].中小学英语教学与研究，2015(09)：19-23.

[9] 张菊荣.“教—学—评一致性”：从方案设计到课堂实施[J].江苏教育，2017(26)：29-31.

[10] 中华人民共和国教育部.普通高中英语课程标准(2017 年版 2020 年修订)[S].北京：人民教育出版社，2020.

案例 5

以"写"为导向的高三英语听、说、读、写"四位一体"线上教学案例

【摘　要】 本篇文章是以"写"为导向的高三英语听、说、读、写"四位一体"线上教学案例，听力材料取自上海市嘉定区 2021 学年高三英语一模试卷，讲述青少年参与社区志愿者活动的意义。教学对象是已具备一定听力技巧和口头表达能力的高三学生。教师在网络教学环境下，引入话题，激活思维；学习听力技巧，落实听力训练；扫读文本，核对听力，厘清文本框架；听、说结合，搭建写作支架；完成写作提纲，实现从输入到输出的思维提升；最终达成提升学生核心素养的目的。

【关键词】 听、说、读、写；高中英语写作；线上教学

一、教学内容分析

听力材料取自上海市嘉定区 2021 学年高三英语一模试卷，讲述青少年参与社区志愿者活动的意义，这是一份培养学生社会责任感的理想材料。本书课旨在将听、说、读、写结合起来，让学生通过聆听、讨论参与社区志愿者活动的意义，表达自己的感受，最终践行社会责任担当。

二、学情分析

本节课的教学对象为川沙中学高三年级的学生，该阶段的学生正在进行历年各区模拟试卷的练习，具备一定的听力技巧和口头表达能力。但是，在从听到说以及从说到写的思维转换过程中，他们仍然缺失思维支架。

三、教学目标

1. 运用预测法等听力技巧完成听力练习，准确获取听力文本的中心思想和细节；

2. 利用听力材料，通过小组合作的方式交流社区志愿者的经历和感受，完成从听到说的能力转换；

3. 基于听、读、说三个环节的积累，能构思写作思维导图，为后续写作产出搭建支架。

四、教学重难点

重点：引导学生完成听—读—说—写这样一个层层递进的思维提升过程，并在该过程中培养英语学科核心素养。

难点：在网络教学环境下，充分调动学生积极参与听、说、读、写各个环节的课堂交流和评价，并对学生生成的内容进行有效的指导。

五、教学流程

任务一：引入话题，激活思维

学　生　活　动	目　　的	技术手段
观看在上海疫情期间，社区志愿者们同心抗疫、无私奉献的图片，并回答相关问题： (1) 他们是谁？ (2) 他们在做什么？ (3) 他们为什么要这么做？	1. 激发学生对社区志愿者这一听力文本主题的兴趣。 2. 唤醒学生已有的知识，为后续的口语和写作做铺垫。	在钉钉群共享抗疫影像。

任务二：学习听力技巧，落实听力训练

学　生　活　动	目　　的	技术手段
1. 观看“空中课堂”片段，学习听力答题技巧。 2. 根据听力选项预测听力内容，听文本并完成听力题。	1. 帮助学生掌握预测、精听等听力技巧。 2. 完成听力训练并掌握听力文本的中心思想和细节。	1. 教师屏幕共享“空中课堂”片段。 2. 学生观看视频后下载听力材料，完成听力题。

任务三：扫读文本，核对听力，厘清文本框架

学 生 活 动	目　　的	技 术 手 段
1. 快速扫读听力文本，圈画主题句和关键字词，根据文本纠正听力选项答案。 2. 和小组同学互相核查听力选项，跟随教师一起核对答案，完成听力任务。	1. 听、读结合，帮助学生快速找到文本的重要信息。 2. 合作学习，分享观点并落实正确答案。	1. 教师点名请学生开麦回答所选答案，并要求学生陈述理由。 2. 学生利用钉钉小组群分组讨论。 3. 学生可以在互动区留言或开麦向教师提问。

任务四：听、说结合，搭建写作支架

学 生 活 动	目　　的	技 术 手 段
1. 小组进行口语交流：讲述自己曾经参与过的志愿者活动，以及参与志愿者活动带来的启发。 2. 小组共同完成“benefits of being a volunteer”的思维导图，罗列论点和论据。	1. 引导学生在主题语境下，联系自己的生活体验，进行观点的分享和思维的碰撞。 2. 概括观点，为写作输出搭建支架，并在思想交流中建立积极的人生观、价值观。	1. 学生分组讨论后，选出代表进行发言，分享观点。 2. 小组通过屏幕分享完成的思维导图。 3. 学生在群里投票选出优秀的小组作品。

任务五：完成写作提纲，实现从输入到输出的思维提升

学 生 活 动	目　　的	技 术 手 段
1. 基于听、说和思维导图，独立完成一个和社会志愿者相关的作文提纲。 2. 根据评价标准，小组交流作文提纲，并推选优秀作品。	1. 学生整理思路，完成从听、说到写作的产出过程，实现思维品质的飞跃。 2. 引导学生学会利用评价标准来检验学习成效，学会欣赏优秀作品。	1. 小组代表通过屏幕共享自己的作品。 2. 利用批注、屏幕分享的方式展示优秀作品。

作业：梳理所学，完善习作

课　后　作　业	技　术　手　段
根据课堂所学和写作提纲，完成并润色文章。	学生拍照上传至平台，教师批阅并挑选优秀作文在平台上共享展示。

六、教学说明

1. 整合线上线下教学资源，听、说、读、写“四位一体”，提升学习成效

好的写作素材来源于生活。上海疫情肆虐期间，学校组织开展线上教学，而无数志愿者奋战在一线守护我们的健康、照料我们的生活。嘉定区2021学年一模试卷的听力刚好是一篇关于“担任社区志愿者会给我们带来哪些收获”的文章，两个主题完美契合。基于此，我们不妨将线上线下的资源合二为一，利用“空中课堂”听力技巧的学习，带领学生从听力过渡到阅读、口语，最终实现写作的产出。在这“四位一体”的过程中，教师通过层层递进的思维挖掘，帮助学生形成积极参与社区志愿者活动的意识，提升学生的社会责任感，落实学生核心素养的培养。

2. 网络教学，扬长避短，丰富教学手段，共享学习成果

众所周知，网络教学确实存在不足，但是它有自身的优势。我们教师不妨扬长避短，善假于物，这样它便能成为我们手中的魔法棒，丰富教学手段，带给学生惊喜，师生共享学习成果。本节课充分利用观看“空中课堂”视频、钉钉屏幕共享、在线批注、连麦交流等方式，为学生打通交流的渠道；通过分组讨论和共享点评，鼓励学生口头表达自己的观点，并在制作思维导图的过程中集思广益，在写作提纲中获得体验感。

最重要的是，通过本节课的学习，学生完成了听、说、读、写“四位一体”的综合训练，并且提升了积极参与社区志愿者活动的意识，树立了社会担当，培养了家国情怀，有助于实现教育立德树人根本任务。

案例 6

“双新”背景下近两年上海高考英语作文题解析及教学建议

【摘　要】 课程标准指出高中英语学科核心素养包括语言能力、思维品质、文化意识和学习能力。这些素养指导了高考英语作文命题的设计和内容，对教学起着重要的引导作用。在新课标的引领下，新教材为我们提供了很多与生活息息相关的话题和语言素材。本文将以“双新”为背景，从核心素养考试评价角度简要分析近两年上海高考英语作文题，从而探讨如何有效地进行高中英语写作的教与学。

【关键词】 “双新”；核心素养；高考英语写作；考试评价

一、引言

1. “双新”的内涵

“双新”指的是新课程、新教材。这是以学生为中心的教育观的体现，强调育人为先，培养学生的核心素养，让学习真正地发生。它是一项系统化措施，涉及新课程方案、新课程标准、新教材、新教学方式、新评价机制和新高考（中考）等方面，旨在促进学校在教育理念、教育内容、教学方式、师生关系等方面进行内源性变革。

2. 新课程和高考英语写作之间的关系

《普通高中英语课程标准（2017 年版 2020 年修订）》指出，学科核心素养是学科育人价值的集中体现，是学生通过学科学习而逐步形成的正确价值观、必备品格和关键能力。高中英语核心素养是指学生在高中英语学习过程中应该具备的核心能力和基本知识，它包括了语言能力、思维品质、文化意识和学习能力四个维度。

高考英语写作与核心素养关系紧密。英语写作是考查学生综合运用英语语言能力的重要环节。首先，语言能力是英语写作的基础，只有具备扎实的语法和词汇基础，学生才能正确、流畅地表达自己的思想。其次，学生思维品质对于英语写作也至关重要。学生只有通过在写作中合理运用逻辑思维、批判性思维甚

至是创新性思维，才能让自己的文章更具有说服力和影响力。再次，学生在高考英语作文中展现的文化意识也会影响作文的质量。学生通过了解与话题相关的文化背景和社会问题，可以丰富论据和观点。最后，学习能力对于学生高考英语作文成绩的提高也非常重要。学生需要掌握高效的学习方法和策略，在备考过程中逐渐提高自己的写作水平和技巧。在近年来的上海英语高考作文题中，对学生学习能力的要求也有所体现。

3. 新教材和高考英语写作之间的关系

从2020年开始使用的高中英语新教材（上教版）为学生的写作搭建了一个非常丰富的学习平台。首先，通过每个板块中的听、说、读、写，学生们可以积累大量的话题和语言素材；其次，新教材中"写"的部分，不仅注重培养学生的论证能力和写作技巧，还非常注重培养学生的思辨能力和创新意识；最后，新教材的写作部分，通过创设真实的情境，培养学生解决实际问题的能力。这些都与高考英语写作的要求高度一致。

二、近两年上海高考英语作文题解析

从2020年开始，上海全面铺开新课程，2023年为使用新课程的高考元年，2024年为第二年。笔者通过整理、汇总这两年的上海英语高考作文真题，从解析命题思路、对标新课标和上教版新教材入手，得出了一些体会和感悟，在此给教师们提供一些启发和教学建议。

年份	高考英语作文真题	对标新课程学科核心素养	对标新教材话题和语篇	对标新教材写作要求和技巧
2024年春考	假如你是明启中学高三学生李华，你的学校邀请文学教授来你校进行文学讲座，由你负责联系。信件内容如下，请你按照内容写一封回信。 Dear Li Hua, Thanks for	1. 需要学生具有扎实的语言能力，能够流畅、准确地写回信。 2. 需要学生具有一定的文化意识，对英美文学有一定的认知和感悟，使得所提出的问题更为翔实并真实可信。还需要学	本作文属于"人与社会"这一主题，要求学生对于英美文学有一定的了解，并就此提出合理的问题：在英美文学方面，有哪些是中国学生感兴趣的问题？ 在上教版教材的多篇课文中，都出现了有关英美文学	学生需掌握如何写好一封正式的信件以及如何提问的语言能力。 必修 第二册 Unit 3 Writing: Writing a formal email to make enquiries about an English

续　表

年份	高考英语作文真题	对标新课程学科核心素养	对标新教材话题和语篇	对标新教材写作要求和技巧
2024年春考	inviting me. For my lecture, I'd like to know what about literature interests Chinese students most. Please give me two questions you'd like to ask and tell me why you choose those two questions. I am looking forward to your reply.	生有跨文化交流的能力，对所写回信具有一定的读者意识。 3. 需要学生具有清晰的逻辑思维、批判性思维和创新性思维，能够有创造性地提出个性化的两个问题，并就为什么提出这两个问题进行有逻辑的论证。 4. 需要学生展现一定的学习能力，学习能力不仅仅体现在日常的学习中，“会提问题”也是学习能力重要的外在体现。	的课文，如： 必修 第二册 Unit 4 Reading: An excerpt from *The Old Man and the Sea* 选择性必修 第一册 Unit 4 Reading: An excerpt from *A Walk in the Woods* 选择性必修 第二册 Unit 4 Reading: “The Last Leaf” 可见，高考真题的话题并非信手拈来，新教材为学生提供了很多话题和语言素材。	course in the UK 可见，新教材同样为我们提供了高考真题的写作要求和技巧的指导。
2023年秋考	假如你是明启中学高三学生吴磊，你校英语节即将举行主题为“快乐童年”的展览，邀请每位同学提供一件生活中的物品参展，并撰写展品介绍供参观者阅读。你会提供什么物品？写一篇物品介绍，内容须包括： 1. 对该物品的简要描述； 2. 你选择该物品参展的原因。	1. 需要学生具有扎实的语言能力对该参展物品进行简要描述并阐述选择该物品参展的原因。 2. 需要学生具有逻辑思维进行合理的论证，清晰地阐述原因。 3. 需要学生具有创新性思维，如果学生选择的物品具有新意，又有充分合理的原因，则该文章可以获得高分。	本作文属于“人与社会”和“人与自我”这两个主题，既要求学生关注学校中的各类活动，又要关注自己的童年经历。在上教版教材中多处出现相关内容，如： 选择性必修 第三册 Unit 2 Listening: Creating an exhibit Speaking: Selecting exhibits to display at a museum	需要学生掌握描述事物的语言能力和技巧 必修 第一册 Unit 4 Writing: Writing an article to describe a room 必修 第三册 Unit 2 Writing: Writing an article describing a process 选择性必修 第三册 Unit 1 Writing: Writing a description of a place

续　表

年份	高考英语作文真题	对标新课程学科核心素养	对标新教材话题和语篇	对标新教材写作要求和技巧
2023年春考	假设你是明启中学高三学生李华，你班的英语口语外教Tom希望改变学生上课互动不积极的情况，委托你了解同学的想法。你与全班同学沟通交流后，发现有些同学对课上讨论的话题不感兴趣，有些同学怕犯错，不敢开口。给Tom写一封邮件，在邮件中你必须： 1. 简述同学们的反馈； 2. 向Tom提出改进建议并说明理由。	1. 需要学生具有扎实的语言能力以准确流畅地写回信。 2. 要求学生具有清晰的逻辑思维能力，能够发现问题，提出合理的建议并说明理由。 3. 在日常学习中，鼓励学生主动观察并积极参与学校各类活动，以此丰富生活体验，并能够思考通过什么方式能提升自己的英语口语能力，这属于英语学科核心素养中的学习能力。 4. 需要学生有一定的读者意识，清晰写信的对象为外教，并选择合适的书写口吻。	本作文属于“人与社会”这一主题，既要求学生关注教育教学活动，又要求学生善于发现问题并解决问题。可以在上教版教材中找到以下相关课文： 必修 第二册 Unit 2 Reading：An experiment in education 选择性必修 第三册 Unit 1 Reading：Making school meaningful	需要学生掌握如何提出建议或解决方案的语言及写作技巧。 必修 第三册 Unit 3 Speaking：Giving suggestions on being streetwise 选择性必修 第二册 Unit 3 Writing：Writing a review of a school event 选择性必修 第四册 Unit 3 Speaking：Talking about the best solution to food shortages

三、高考写作命题思路

通过研究近两年的高考真题，笔者总结出了上海英语高考写作的命题思路。

1. *融合“双新”理念与核心素养*

高考英语写作紧密结合新课程和新教材的理念，注重培养学生的核心素养和实际应用能力。新课程提供了丰富的话题和情境，新课标则强调学生的语言能力、文化意识、思维品质和学习能力等核心素养的培养。高考英语写作将这些理念融入题目，通过设计具有实际应用价值的任务，让学生在解决问题的过程中展示他们的核心素养和综合能力。

2. 强调跨文化交流与国际视野

高考英语写作强调跨文化交流和国际视野的培养。特别是2024年的春考作文题中融入了多元文化，引导学生理解不同文化背景下的思维方式和表达方式，培养他们的跨文化交流能力。通过与国际接轨的话题和情境设置，帮助学生拓宽视野，增强国际竞争力。

3. 关注学生的真实感受与主体表达

高考英语写作关注学生的真实感受与主体表达。题目设计充分考虑学生的情感体验和认知特点，鼓励他们真实、准确地表达自己的观点和感受。通过让学生参与讨论、发表意见等方式，培养他们的主体性和独立思考能力。

4. 注重情境设置的真实性与创新性

高考英语写作强调情境设置的真实性和创新性。题目设计结合新课程提供的实际情境，设计具有真实性和可操作性的任务，让学生在真实的语境中运用英语进行思考、表达及解决实际问题。同时，情境设置的创新性也能激发学生的学习兴趣和创造力，鼓励他们从不同的角度思考问题，提出独特的观点和解决方案。

四、教学启示

在“双新”背景下，通过解析近两年的高考真题并加以反思，笔者总结出以下教学建议。

1. 注重语言基础，培养扎实语言能力

面对高考英语作文多样化的要求，教师们首先要重视学生基础语言能力的培养。扎实的语言能力是学生准确表达观点、流畅书写作文的基础。在日常教学中，教师应注重词汇的积累、语法规则的掌握以及句型结构的多样化等练习。例如，可以组织学生进行词汇竞赛，在平时的课文中积累主题词汇，通过游戏化的方式增加词汇量；同时，通过句子翻译、作文改写等练习，帮助学生熟悉并掌握各种句型结构，提高表达的准确性和丰富性。

2. 创设真实情境，发展实际应用能力

高考英语写作强调情境设置的真实性和创新性，因此，教师在教学中应创设真实的语言情境，让学生在模拟的实际环境中进行语言实践。例如，教师可以在平时的教学中，拟一个国际文化交流活动的场景，让学生扮演不同国家的代表，用英语进行交流和讨论。这样的活动不仅能激发学生的学习兴趣，还能帮助他们更好地理解和运用英语，提高实际应用能力。

3. 融入核心素养，深化英语写作教学

新课程强调学生的核心素养培养，包括语言能力、文化意识、思维品质和学习能力等方面。在英语写作教学中，教师应将核心素养的培养融入其中，通过有针对性的教学活动，帮助学生提升这些方面的能力。例如，在教授写作的过程中，教师应注重培养学生的逻辑思维能力，引导他们有条理地组织观点；在解读作文题目时，教师可以引导学生关注文化因素，培养跨文化意识；同时，教师还可以鼓励学生自主学习，通过查阅资料和讨论，拓展写作思路，提升学习能力。

4. 结合新教材，丰富英语写作素材

新教材为英语写作教学提供了丰富的话题内容，包括科技、文化、环境、社会、学校、教育等多个方面。在写作教学中，教师应充分利用这些话题内容，为学生提供多样化的写作素材，激发他们的写作兴趣。教师可以根据新教材的话题内容，系统性地建立主题词汇语言库，设计相关的写作任务，引导学生关注社会热点、思考现实问题，培养他们的社会责任感和批判性思维。如在学习选择性必修第三册 Unit 1 时，主课文为 Making school meaningful, Mini-project 为 Improving the school curriculum。此单元中的听说板块同样与校园生活有关，因此教师可以引导学生建立和学校教育相关的语料库，语料库应包含本课中的词汇和句型结构，也可通过小组合作等形式进行拓展。教师还可以校园或教育为话题，出一些相关的作文题。

五、结语

在“双新”背景下，高考英语作文命题日益注重核心素养的培养与实际应用能力的提升，课堂教学也应调整策略。教师要夯实学生语言基础，创设真实情境，让学生在模拟环境中实践，提升英语应用水平。此外，还需融入核心素养培养，强化逻辑思维、文化意识和自主学习能力。只有通过这些培养路径和教学策略，我们才能真正达成立德树人的目标，才能培养出符合新时代发展要求的优秀人才。

参考文献

[1] 高惠蓉，等.“双新”背景下的中学英语语篇教学新探索[M].上海：上海交通

大学出版社，2021.
[2] 上海市中小学（幼儿园）课程改革委员会.普通高中教科书　英语　必修　第一册[M].上海：上海教育出版社，2020.
[3] 上海市中小学（幼儿园）课程改革委员会.普通高中教科书　英语　必修　第二册[M].上海：上海教育出版社，2020.
[4] 上海市中小学（幼儿园）课程改革委员会.普通高中教科书　英语　必修　第三册[M].上海：上海教育出版社，2020.
[5] 上海市中小学（幼儿园）课程改革委员会.普通高中教科书　英语　必修　第四册[M].上海：上海教育出版社，2020.
[6] 上海市中小学（幼儿园）课程改革委员会.普通高中教科书　英语　选择性必修　第一册[M].上海：上海教育出版社，2020.
[7] 上海市中小学（幼儿园）课程改革委员会.普通高中教科书　英语　选择性必修　第二册[M].上海：上海教育出版社，2020.
[8] 上海市中小学（幼儿园）课程改革委员会.普通高中教科书　英语　选择性必修　第三册[M].上海：上海教育出版社，2020.
[9] 上海市中小学（幼儿园）课程改革委员会.普通高中教科书　英语　选择性必修　第四册[M].上海：上海教育出版社，2020.
[10] 中华人民共和国教育部.普通高中英语课程标准（2017 年版 2020 年修订）[S].北京：人民教育出版社，2020.

CHAPTER 05

第五章　范文参考

第一节　议论文

第二节　应用文

第三节　记叙文

第一节 议 论 文

一、图片类作文

(一) 范文示例

2002 年上海高考作文

简要描述图片内容，结合生活实际，就图片的主题谈谈自己的感想。

你们让我自己骑好吗？

As is vividly depicted in the picture, a young girl is riding a bike, with almost all her family members around, in case anything unexpected should happen.【简要描述图片内容】

It's a common phenomenon that parents care too much about their children.【揭示图片的主题】As far as I am concerned, it's not sensible for parents to overprotect their children. My reasons are listed as follows.【简要阐述自己的观点】

First and foremost, overprotected children may lack the essential life skills required for adulthood.【主题句】Shielded from challenges, they grow up without experiencing failure, which is essential for character building and resilience. Consequently, they may struggle to adapt to real-world situations and might become dependent on others.

Additionally, a lack of independence may hinder their decision-making abilities and personal growth.【主题句】For example, a college graduate, who has just left school, is admitted into an enterprise, can meet with a lot of new things every day, which needs his decision-making. What if he never makes decisions by himself? Can he ask for help or advice again in his company? Of course not! It is independence that he needs to learn from childhood.

Therefore, overprotection of children by Chinese parents, though well-

intentioned, has its drawbacks. Only by striking a balance between parental guidance and allowing children to experience challenges, can parents raise independent, self-reliant individuals who are better prepared to face the complexities of life.

好词好句：

1. As is vividly depicted in the picture ... 如图所示……（as 引导的非限制性定语从句）

2. ... in case anything unexpected should happen. ……以防万一出现意外。（in case 引导的条件状语从句）

3. ... it's not sensible for parents to overprotect their children. ……父母过度保护孩子是不明智的。（It be＋形容词＋for sb. to do sth.句型）

4. Shielded from challenges, they grow up without experiencing failure, which is essential for character building and resilience. 由于没有挑战，他们在成长过程中没有经历过失败，而失败对塑造性格和韧性至关重要。（通过 shielded 非谓语结构和主从复合句表达观点）

shield from 防护，保护

resilience *n*. 韧性

5. ... a lack of independence may hinder their decision-making abilities and personal growth. ……缺乏独立性可能会抑制他们的决策力和个人成长。（用 a lack of independence 名词性短语表达观点）

hinder *v*. 阻碍，打扰

6. For example, a college graduate, who has just left school, is admitted into an enterprise, can meet with a lot of new things every day ... 例如，一个刚毕业的大学生，被一家企业录取了，每天都能遇到很多新事物……（通过举例法进行分析）

7. What if he never makes decisions by himself? Can he ask for help or advice again in his company? Of course not! 如果他从不自己做决定怎么办？他能在公司里再次寻求帮助或建议吗？当然不能！（通过两个问句引出答案，从而加强语气）

8. Only by striking a balance between parental guidance and allowing

children to experience challenges, can parents raise independent, self-reliant individuals ... 只有在父母的指导和让孩子经历挑战之间取得平衡,父母才能培养出独立的、自力更生的个体……(Only+介词短语位于句首引起的部分倒装)

点评

文章结构为总—分—总。第一、第二段为文章第一部分,描述图片内容、揭示图片的主题、阐明观点。开门见山,主旨清晰。第三、第四段为文章的第二部分,阐述了作者认为过度保护孩子的不明智之处,共两个原因。第二个原因使用了举例法加以分析,做到了两个层次详略得当。第五段为文章的第三部分,总结全文,提出建议。

文章结构清晰,主旨明确,合理使用了主题句,并通过举例法加以分析,详略得当,内容充实,语言丰富,句型多变,是一篇优秀的图片类作文。

(二) 实战演练

2012 年上海高考作文

上周一,你在一所小学观摩了小女孩 Amy 所在班级的两堂绘画课(如图所示),回家后你用英语写了一篇日记,内容包括:

- 对两堂绘画课的具体描述;
- 你从中获得的启发。

My Diary

Monday, May 28th

Today, I paid a visit to a primary school where a girl named Amy studies to observe 2 art lessons. In the first class, the teacher presented everyone with a large piece of paper and required them to paint whatever they liked on it. So excited was Amy that she applied the colours to her feet, using them as paint brushes. In the other class, on the contrary, the teacher just instructed them to copy the model painting. Despite the fact that Amy also painted her pictures earnestly, I discovered that she wasn't involved in the painting as passionately. I maintain it was the creativity and imagination that made the striking difference between the 2 classes.

First and foremost, what impressed me most was Amy's sweet smile in the first class. 【主题句】It goes without saying that the happiness from one's creation and imagination will allow him to receive the real sense of achievement and satisfaction from his work. Only when we feel pleased with our works can we create something brilliant.

Simultaneously, equipped with innovation spirit, we will be more likely to develop our potential abilities. Given that every one of us say the same words or do the same things, our country will be destined to become less dynamic and prosperous. However, it is a fair bet that more amazing contributions will be achieved with our initiative.

As mentioned above, I firmly hold the belief that creativity and imagination are two invaluable qualities which success feeds on. Therefore, I will go to any length to cultivate my creativity and imagination to make greater contributions to my country.

好词好句：

1. So excited was Amy that she applied the colours to her feet, using them as paint brushes.艾米非常兴奋，她把这些颜色涂在自己的脚上，把它们作为画笔。(使用了一个So+形容词位于句首引起的部分倒装)

apply ... to ... 涂抹，贴；适用于；运用；向……申请(要求)；致力于

2. Despite the fact that Amy also painted her pictures earnestly, I discovered that she wasn't involved in the painting as passionately. 尽管艾米也认真地画了她的画,但我发现她并没有那么热情地投入这幅画。(使用了 despite the fact that ...这种较为复杂的结构来替换 though ...,体现了语言的丰富性)

earnestly *adv.* 认真地,诚挚地,热切地

3. I maintain it was the creativity and imagination that made the striking difference between the 2 classes. 我认为是创造力和想象力使这两个班级之间产生了显著的差异。(使用了 it 引导的强调句型,强调创造力和想象力的重要性)

maintain that ... 坚持认为……

the striking difference 显著的差异

4. Only when we feel pleased with our works can we create something brilliant.只有当我们对自己的作品感到满意时,我们才能创造出辉煌。(使用了 only 修饰状语从句位于句首引起的部分倒装)

5. Simultaneously, equipped with innovation spirit, we will be more likely to develop our potential abilities. 同时,拥有创新精神,我们将更有可能开发我们的潜在能力。(使用了 equipped 非谓语做伴随状语)

simultaneously *adv.* 同时地

点评

本题为2012年高考作文真题,要求学生写一篇日记,先简单描述两幅图片,然后发表自己的观点。需要运用到写作技巧中的对比法和描写法。

本篇文章第一段通过对比的方式简单描述了两幅图片。第二和第三段从两个层次阐述了自己从中获得的启发。尾段先对上文进行总结,然后立志要努力培养创造力和想象力来为祖国做贡献,升华了文章的主题。文章结构清晰,体现了日记的形式,词汇和句型结构比较丰富。

二、图表类作文

(一) 范文示例①

上周你校进行了谁是你的偶像的调查。得出结果如表格所示。请简要描述调查结果，并对此发表自己的看法。

偶　　像	男　　生	女　　生
影视明星	18%	51%
体育明星	48%	7%
科学家、英雄	20%	18%
父母	7%	22%
无偶像	7%	2%

As indicated in the table, the majority of students exhibit a fascination with idols. Approximately half of the boys express interest in sports stars, while 51% of girls admire movie stars. More than one-third of students look up to scientists and heroes. However, only seven percent of boys and twenty-two percent of girls choose their parents as their idols.【简要描述图表内容，不需要所有数据面面俱到，但要抓住核心问题】

It is a common phenomenon to typically define idols as attractive individuals. Nevertheless, the true essence of an idol, as far as I am concerned, is anyone who motivates, imparts wisdom about life, and has a positive impact on us.【引出现象，并定义偶像】

In my opinion, parents fulfill these criteria exceptionally well.【主题句】We often come across others saying, "those movie stars or sports icons

① "范文示例"部分的作文题目来自詹玲：《高考英语写作专项训练》，上海教育出版社，2010，第 93 页。

inspired me during my lowest moments" or "I fear being isolated because I don't follow popular idols." However, I believe that idols should be those individuals who have had the most significant influence on us. It is our parents who have witnessed every moment of our growth. It is our parents who have patiently guided and inspired us through difficult times. So, why not consider them as our idols when they have devoted so much to helping us?

The choices of idols vary from person to person, but I strongly advocate for viewing our parents as our idols. After all, they have truly been helpful in making our lives better.【通过呼吁总结全文】

好词好句：

1. Approximately half of the boys express interest in sports stars, while 51% of girls admire movie stars. 大约有一半的男孩表示对体育明星感兴趣，而51%的女孩则欣赏影视明星。（通过 while 对比前后两组数据，用不同的词汇表达喜欢，展现了词汇的多样性）

approximately *adv.* 大概；大约

express interest in sports stars 对体育明星感兴趣

admire *v.* 欣赏；赞美，钦佩

2. Nevertheless, the true essence of an idol, as far as I am concerned, is anyone who motivates, imparts wisdom about life, and has a positive impact on us. 然而，一个偶像的真正本质，在我看来，是任何一个激励、传授生活的智慧，并对我们产生积极影响的人。（通过一个定语从句定义偶像，为下文的展开做铺垫）

essence *n.* 本质，实质

impart *v.* 传授；给予；告知

3. It is our parents who have witnessed every moment of our growth. It is our parents who have patiently guided and inspired us through difficult times. 是我们的父母见证了我们成长的每一刻。是我们的父母耐心地引导和激励我们度过困难时期。（通过两个强调句进行情感渲染，体现父母的重要性）

4. So, why not consider them as our idols when they have devoted so much to helping us? 所以，为什么不把他们当作我们的偶像，当他们已经投入了这么多来帮助我们？（通过一个反问句，建议大家以父母为偶像）

点评

第一段，简要描述图表内容，抓住了核心问题。第二段，引出现象，并定义偶像，为下文做铺垫。第三段，首句为主题句，引出作者的观点，认为父母是值得我们尊敬的偶像，并展开论述；在论述中使用了强调句型以加强感情色彩。第四段，通过呼吁总结全文。整篇文章结构严谨，层层递进，逻辑清晰，语言丰富，是一篇值得借鉴的优秀文章。

（二）实战演练

2021 年"青少年网红梦"一度成为全国热点讨论话题。作为一名高中生，请根据"2021 年毕业生求职意向调查报告"显示的数据（见下表），谈谈你对该话题的看法并给出理由。

最受欢迎职业前三名：

主播(anchor)	25.12%
网红[influencer/KOL (Key Opinion Leader)]	19.06%
新媒体运营专员(new media operation specialist)	18.20%

（注：文中不得出现真实的姓名及学校名称。）

Becoming Internet celebrities has become the dream job for millions of teenagers, a trend attracting nationwide attention. According to a survey among college graduates in 2021, being an anchor on live-streaming platforms takes the lead, accounting for 25.12% of the respondents. The choices of becoming influencers and new media operation specialists follow closely behind, making up 19.06% and 18.20% respectively.

For anyone paying attention, these results should come as no shock.【主题句】With social media platforms accessible to everyone, some teenagers find a way to get attention and attract followers, translating fame into fortune. No wonder so many harbour dreams of Internet celebrity.【分析现象背后的原因】

However, I don't believe this is an ideal career path for everyone, especially teenagers who lack rational judgement to chart their own course.【主题句】Truth be told, it is not easy to make it in the business. Given the increasingly fierce competition, players will have to work extra hard on their contents and develop strategies to market themselves, sometimes even at the risk of their privacy. And remember it is not just upload and forget, you have to promote your content every day and make more appealing videos. Moreover, obsession with online celebrity may be detrimental to teenagers' growth in the long term. Living under the illusion of instant success, some may lose the motivation to study and thus fail to invest in meaningful things.

Therefore, instead of following the trend blindly, it's advisable for us teenagers to remain cool-headed and adopt a down-to-earth attitude to life. Only by doing so can we truly form a clearer vision of ourselves and explore a career path that best suits us and brings our talent into full play.

好词好句：

1. According to a survey among college graduates in 2021, being an anchor on live-streaming platforms takes the lead, accounting for 25.12% of the respondents. 根据一项针对2021年高校毕业生的调查，想成为直播平台的主播的人数最多，占受访者的25.12%。（accounting 非谓语结构做伴随状语）

live-streaming platforms 直播平台

take the lead 领先

2. Given the increasingly fierce competition, players will have to work extra hard on their contents and develop strategies to market themselves, sometimes even at the risk of their privacy. 考虑到日益激烈的竞争，平台玩家们不得不更加努力地处理自己的内容，并制定策略来推销自己，有时甚至会冒着个人隐私泄露的风险。

Given ... 考虑到，鉴于……

work extra hard on sth. 更加努力地做某事

3. Moreover, obsession with online celebrity may be detrimental to teenagers' growth in the long term. 此外，从长远来看，对网红的痴迷可能会不

利于青少年的成长。(obsession with online celebrity 名词词组做主语)

obsession with online celebrity 对网红痴迷

be detrimental to 有害于;对……不利

4. Only by doing so can we truly form a clearer vision of ourselves and explore a career path that best suits us and brings our talent into full play. 只有这样做,我们才能真正形成一个更清晰的自我愿景,探索一条适合自己、能充分发挥自己才能的职业道路。[only 修饰状语(或状语从句)位于句首引起的部分倒装]

bring our talent into full play 充分发挥我们的才能

点评

第一段,简要引入"青少年网红梦"的现象,并通过简明扼要的语言分析了相关数据。第二段,通过一个主题句,引出该现象背后的原因。第三段,通过一个主题句,鲜明地亮出作者对此现象不认可的观点,即文章的主旨,并从两方面阐述原因。最后一段,通过呼吁青少年建立正确的职业观念,并给出两个建议来结束全文。整篇文章审题准确,观点鲜明,结构清晰,词汇运用得准确且娴熟,是一篇不可多得的佳作。

三、现象类作文

(一) 范文示例

如今微信(WeChat)走进了人们的生活,为大家带来了诸多便利,但有些人也随之成了"微信控"(WeChataholic)。请你就此事写一篇文章,文章须包括:

1. 对此现象的描述;
2. 你对"微信控"的看法。

It is widely recognized that WeChat has significantly influenced our daily life, providing us with immense convenience. However, so obssessed are some individuals with this technology that they have become virtually WeChataholic. As far as I am concerned, I am strongly opposed to this behaviour.【主旨句】

One significant reason lies in that it can lead to a lack of face-to-face communication.【主题句】As a consequence, they may find it difficult to establish meaningful relationships with others in the real world.

Furthermore, WeChataholic often results in a considerable waste of time, which is another factor contributing to my disapproval.【主题句】For instance, we can often find some of our classmates, who tend to lack self-discipline, becoming hooked on WeChat. They find it challenging to resist the urge to constantly check their phones when doing their homework. This distraction can significantly impair their focus on studies, thus leading to their poor academic performance.

Therefore, it is crucial to use WeChat responsibly and avoid becoming overly dependent on it. Otherwise, our lives may become chaotic and unbalanced. Only by striking a balance between technology and real-world interactions can we ensure that WeChat remains a valuable tool rather than a hindrance to our well-being.

好词好句：

1. However, so obssessed are some individuals with this technology that they have become virtually WeChataholic. 然而，有些人对这项技术如此着迷，以至于他们几乎变成了微信控。(运用了"so +形容词+……+that 从句"的结构：so 修饰形容词放在句首，主句部分倒装)

be obssessed with ... 着迷于……

virtually *adv*. 事实上；几乎；虚拟地

2. Furthermore, WeChataholic often results in a considerable waste of time, which is another factor contributing to my disapproval. 此外，微信控经常会浪费大量时间，这是我反对的另一个原因。(运用了 which 引导的非限制性定语从句和 contributing 非谓语结构)

3. This distraction can significantly impair their focus on studies, thus leading to their poor academic performance. 这种分心会严重削弱他们对学习的关注度，从而导致他们的学习成绩不佳。(运用了 leading 非谓语结构做结果状语)

impair *vt*. 损害，削弱

4. Only by striking a balance between technology and real-world

interactions can we ensure that WeChat remains a valuable tool rather than a hindrance to our well-being. 只有在技术和现实世界的互动之间取得平衡，我们才能确保微信仍然是一个有价值的工具，而不是对我们幸福健康的一种阻碍。[only 修饰状语（或状语从句）位于句首引起的部分倒装]

hindrance *n.* 阻碍，妨碍；障碍物

点评

本文为现象类文章。文章结构为：第一段，引入现象；第二段，发表自己对此现象的观点；第三段和第四段从两个方面论证自己的观点，并做到了有详有略，在第四段中通过一个身边的实例来论证本段的主题句；第五段，先重申主旨，再通过一个"Only by doing ..."的句式来总结全文。全文句式多变，语言丰富，内容完整，是一篇不错的范文。

（二）实战演练

据新闻报道，国庆长假全国各地景点游客爆满，比如杭州仅假期第三天接待的游客量就高达 100 万人次。此新闻引发了人们对长假的不同看法。你在日记中写下了你的感受。日记内容包括：

1. 对新闻的简要描述；
2. 你的感受和建议。

This morning, while browsing the Internet, I came across a news article that caught my attention. It stated that West Lake, as reported locally, received a staggering one million visitors on the third day of the National Day holiday alone. In fact, nearly all of China's scenic spots witnessed a strong desire among people to go sightseeing during this week-long holiday.

As far as I am concerned, although the holiday did stimulate tourism and support economic growth, it also brought forth numerous challenges. 【主旨句】

First, the tourist resorts faced immense pressure due to the overwhelming number of visitors. The large crowds not only posed significant threats to public facilities but also endangered the safety of the tourists themselves. Furthermore, the overcrowding made it difficult for tourists to truly enjoy their sightseeing experiences as they had to struggle through the masses to reach the scenic spots.

Given that the seven-day holiday has resulted in more negative consequences than positive outcomes, I believe the government should promptly implement measures to address the current situation. For instance, it is crucial to instil a sense of responsibility among the public in protecting these scenic spots and promote ethical behavior and morality.

好词好句：

1. It stated that West Lake, as reported locally, received a staggering one million visitors on the third day of the National Day holiday alone. 据当地媒体报道，仅在国庆假期的第三天，西湖接待的游客量就达惊人的 100 万人次。（as reported 作为插入语）

staggering *adj*. 令人难以置信的，令人震惊的

2. The tourist resorts faced immense pressure due to the overwhelming number of visitors. 由于游客数量众多，这些旅游胜地面临着巨大的压力。（词汇丰富）

immense *adj*.（尤指规模、程度）巨大的，广大的

overwhelming *adj*. 势不可挡的，压倒的

3. Given that the seven-day holiday has resulted in more negative consequences than positive outcomes, I believe the government should promptly implement measures to address the current situation. 鉴于七天假期造成的负面后果大于积极结果，我认为政府应该立即实施措施来解决目前的情况。（given that 引导原因状语从句）

Given that ... 考虑到这一点……

promptly implement measures 立即实施措施

4. For instance, it is crucial to instil a sense of responsibility among the public in protecting these scenic spots and promote ethical behavior and morality. 例如，给公众灌输保护这些景点的责任感、提升道德行为和道德规范是至关重要的。（it 句型及丰富的词汇）

instil *v.* 逐步灌输，逐步培养（尤指好的思想、态度等）

ethical behavior and morality 道德行为和道德规范

点评

本文为现象类文章，文章结构为：第一段，引入现象；第二段，发表自己对此现象的观点；第三段，指出面临的挑战；第四段，总结、建议。全文结构清晰，内容翔实，逻辑连贯，词汇丰富，并且首段的语言充分体现了这篇文章的体裁为日记。

四、利弊类作文

（一）范文示例

现如今，越来越多家庭开始饲养宠物，请以“The Pros and Cons of Keeping Pets”为题，谈谈饲养宠物的利与弊。

The Pros and Cons of Keeping Pets

In recent years, keeping pets has become increasingly popular among families. While there are many benefits, there are also some drawbacks to consider.

The practice does bring a lot of benefits.【主题句】One advantage of having a pet is the companionship they provide. Pets, such as dogs and cats, can be loyal and loving friends, offering unconditional love and emotional support. They can help reduce feelings of loneliness and provide a sense of security and comfort. More importantly, pets can teach responsibility and empathy. For example, when children raise a pet, they can learn to take care of a pet, feeding, grooming, and creating a safe environment for them. This can instil a sense of duty and compassion in individuals, as the well-being of the pet becomes their responsibility.

However, there are also disadvantages to owning a pet.【主题句】Firstly, pets require a significant investment of time, effort, and money. Regular veterinary check-ups, vaccinations, and dietary needs can be costly. Worse still, pets need regular exercise and attention, which means owners must be prepared to dedicate time to their care. Another detrimental aspect is the potential for health issues. Some individuals may be allergic to pet dander, causing respiratory problems or skin irritations.

As the saying goes, each coin has two sides. Therefore, keeping pets has both pros and cons. As far as I am concerned, we should not be lost in the argument. What we should keep in mind is that it is essential for individuals to make an informed choice based on their individual circumstances and capabilities.

好词好句:

1. Pets, such as dogs and cats, can be loyal and loving friends, offering unconditional love and emotional support. 宠物,如狗和猫,可以成为忠诚和友爱的朋友,能提供无条件的爱和情感支持。(offering 非谓语充当伴随状语)

2. For example, when children raise a pet, they can learn to take care of a pet, feeding, grooming, and creating a safe environment for them. 例如,当孩子们养宠物时,他们可以学习照顾宠物,喂养、梳理毛发,并为它们创造一个安全的环境。(通过举例法说明养宠物可以培养责任感和共情能力)

3. This can instil a sense of duty and compassion in individuals, as the well-being of the pet becomes their responsibility. 这可以向个人灌输一种责任感和同情心,因为宠物的幸福成为他们的责任。

4. Worse still, pets need regular exercise and attention, which means owners must be prepared to dedicate time to their care. 更糟糕的是,宠物需要定期锻炼和关注,这意味着主人必须准备好花时间来照顾它们。(通过非限制性定语从句进行补充说明)

5. Another detrimental aspect is the potential for health issues. 另一个有害的方面是潜在的健康问题。

detrimental *adj*. 有害的;不利的

点评

本篇文章为利弊作文,结构为:第一段,引入"宠物热"这一现象,阐明自己的观点,即有利有弊(主旨);第二段,阐述养宠物的好处;第三段,阐述养宠物的坏处；第四段，总结＋建议。文章结构清晰，利弊分析使用了主题句，通过举例使得内容变得翔实，句型和词汇非常丰富。

（二）实战演练

对中学生穿校服的情况进行调查之后，写一份调查报告。报告须包含以下内容：

1. 多数学生赞成：可避免攀比，有利于学校管理；有人反对：设计单调，不利于个性发展。

2. 谈谈你的看法。

Recently, I have conducted a survey concerning students' school uniforms. Opinions are divided on this issue, as there are both notable advantages and disadvantages.

Supporters argue that school uniforms serve as a tradition with several benefits.【主题句】To begin with, wearing the same clothes eliminates the phenomenon for comparison, thus promoting a healthier mindset among students. Furthermore, uniforms provide convenience for school management. Meanwhile, those holding the opposite view maintain that the disadvantages of school uniforms can't be ignored. The monotonous design and colour can make students feel uninterested in wearing them throughout the year.

Personally, I believe that the disadvantages outweigh the advantages.【主题句】In the first place, the materials which some school uniforms are made of are often far from comfortable, which may cause physical suffering to students. Worse still, the bland design and colour may have a negative impact on students' aesthetic development. Lastly, wearing school uniforms restricts students' freedom and may hinder the development of their personalities, potentially leading to a lack of creativity.

In conclusion, we should relieve the burden of wearing school uniforms on students and allow them more freedom to grow and develop.

好词好句：

1. To begin with, wearing the same clothes eliminates the phenomenon for comparison, thus promoting a healthier mindset among students. 首先，穿同样的衣服消除了比较的现象，从而促进了学生更健康的心态。(thus doing 的结构表结果)

2. Meanwhile, those holding the opposite view maintain that the disadvantages of school uniforms can't be ignored. 与此同时，持反对观点的人认为校服的缺点是不能忽视的。(通过 meanwhile 表示转折；holding 非谓语结构做定语)

3. Personally, I believe that the disadvantages outweigh the advantages. 个人而言，我认为弊大于利。

outweigh *v.* 比……更重要；胜过，强过；比……有价值

4. In the first place, the materials which some school uniforms are made of are often far from comfortable, which may cause physical suffering to students. 首先，一些校服的材料往往很不舒适，这可能会给学生带来身体上的痛苦。(使用了 which 引导的非限制性定语从句)

far from comfortable 远谈不上舒适

点评

第一段开门见山地引入话题，语言简明扼要。第二段根据题目要求，指出"利和弊"两方面，并进行了一定的论证。第三段，作者通过一句主题句清晰地表明自己的观点，即作者认为"弊大于利"，并进行详细阐述。最后一段，简单地总结全文。文章观点明确，结构清晰，语言比较丰富，但如果句型能够更加多变、词汇能更丰富，就更加完美了。

五、选择说理类作文

(一) 范文示例

2013 年上海高考作文

上海博物馆拟举办一次名画展，现就展出场所(博物馆还是社区图书馆)征集公众意见，假设你是王敏，给上海博物馆写一封信表达你的想法。你

的信必须满足以下要求：

1. 简述你写信的目的以及你对场所的选择；

2. 说明你的理由(从便利性、专业性等方面对这两个场所进行对比)。

To someone who may be concerned,

Hearing that an exhibition of famous paintings is going to be held and you are consulting us where to hold it, hardly can I wait to write to share with you my opinion.

I think the Shanghai Museum is the better option. My opinion is easily justified.【清楚地表明自己的选择】

Firstly, in terms of location, the Shanghai Museum is conveniently situated in the city center and is easily accessible through an efficient network of public transportation. In contrast, the community library may pose challenges in terms of accessibility. Holding the exhibition at the Shanghai Museum can ensure that more people have easy access to it, thus increasing the number of individuals exposed to art and enhancing their cultural experiences.

Secondly, the Shanghai Museum boasts advanced facilities and a team of experts, which the community library lacks. By exhibiting the famous paintings at the Shanghai Museum, we can ensure the preservation and protection of these invaluable artworks and allow the museum's experts to provide visitors with insightful and engaging introductions to the paintings. This will undoubtedly broaden the horizons of the attendees and deepen their appreciation for art.

To sum up, I have every reason to choose the Shanghai Museum. I sincerely hope that you will take my opinion into serious consideration. I eagerly anticipate the opportunity to visit the exhibition soon.

Yours sincerely,

Wang Min

好词好句：

1. Hearing that an exhibition of famous paintings is going to be held and

you are consulting us where to hold it, hardly can I wait to write to share with you my opinion. 听说要举办一场名画展览,您方向我们咨询在哪里举办,我迫不及待地想写信与您方分享我的想法。(通过 hearing 非谓语结构开始全文,后面再加上 hardly 位于句首引起的部分倒装结构表明写信的意图)

2. In contrast, the community library may pose challenges in terms of accessibility. 相比之下,社区图书馆可能会在可访问性方面面临挑战。(使用 in contrast 对比前后二者的不同之处)

pose challenges 带来挑战

3. Holding the exhibition at the Shanghai Museum can ensure that more people have easy access to it, thus increasing the number of individuals exposed to art and enhancing their cultural experiences. 在上海博物馆举办展览可以确保更多的人更容易地接触到它,从而增加接触艺术的个人数量,增强他们的文化体验。(increasing 非谓语做结构状语)

4. Secondly, the Shanghai Museum boasts advanced facilities and a team of experts, which the community library lacks. 其次,上海博物馆拥有先进的设施和专家团队,这是社区图书馆所缺乏的。(通过 which 引导的非限制性定语从句表示对比)

boast advanced facilities and a team of experts 拥有先进的设施和专家团队

5. ... provide visitors with insightful and engaging introductions to the paintings. ……为游客提供见解深刻的和迷人的绘画介绍。

insightful *adj*. 富有洞察力的,有深刻见解的

engaging *adj*. 迷人的,有吸引力的

6. I eagerly anticipate the opportunity to visit the exhibition soon. 我热切地期待着很快就能有机会去参观这个展览。

anticipate *v*. 预期;期望

点评

这是 2013 年的上海高考作文题,书信体裁,要求选择开设展览的理想场所并说明选择的原因,要求使用对比法。

此篇文章的结构为：第一段，说明写信事由和意图；第二段，作者的选择；第三、第四段，从位置和专业性两方面进行对比，来论证自己的选择；第五段，总结。整篇文章结构非常清晰，观点明确，合理使用了主题句，通过对比法很好地论证了自己的观点，词汇非常丰富。

（二）实战演练

最近你班同学举行了一次班会，就高三学生如何选择大学专业进行了讨论，并罗列了高三学生选择专业时三个主要的考虑因素：职业前景(career prospect)、个人兴趣(personal interest)和家长的意见(parents' advice)。你考虑的主要因素是哪一个？请做出选择并说明原因。你的文章必须包括：

1. 你的选择；
2. 你做出这个选择的原因。

At a recent class meeting, the topic of choosing a university major was discussed, considering career prospect, personal interest and parents' advice. Among these factors, personal interest takes precedence in my consideration. 【主旨句】

Interest has always been the most powerful motivator, whether in academics or careers. 【主题句】 A genuine passion for one's major and a strong sense of vocation can drive individuals to continually progress. Appreciating the intrinsic value of the work rather than focusing solely on material benefits, tasks are approached with spontaneity and enjoyment, resulting in greater advancements.

Furthermore, interest acts as a source of support during challenging times. 【主题句】 Throughout our lives, we inevitably face obstacles and setbacks. Enthusiasm derived from our interests can illuminate even the darkest nights, while our long-nurtured hopes help alleviate despair. Interest has the power to heal emotional wounds and empower us to overcome adversity.

Moreover, interest nurtures curiosity similar to that of a child. 【主题句】 Cultivating this innate desire to explore the unknown allows individuals to venture into uncharted territories and pave the way for innovation. This, in turn, leads to the realization of our potential and the fulfillment of our values.

While some argue that career prospects guarantee a stable income and a secure future, the reality is that these "promising" majors may change unpredictably. While parental advice undoubtedly offers valuable guidance, ultimately, the decision should be made by ourselves for our own future.

In conclusion, interest serves as the foundation for selecting a major. Without it, we cannot endure the trials, accomplish extraordinary achievements, or revel in our accomplishments.

好词好句：

1. At a recent class meeting, the topic of choosing a university major was discussed, considering career prospect, personal interest and parents' advice. 在最近的一次班会上，我们考虑了职业前景、个人兴趣和家长的意见，讨论了选择大学专业的话题。（considering 非谓语结构充当伴随状语）

2. Enthusiasm derived from our interests can illuminate even the darkest nights, while our long-nurtured hopes help alleviate despair. 从我们的兴趣中产生的热情甚至可以照亮最黑暗的夜晚，而我们长期培养的希望则有助于缓解绝望。（derived 非谓语结构充当定语）

illuminate *v*. 照亮，照明

long-nurtured hopes 长期培养的希望

3. Interest has the power to heal emotional wounds and empower us to overcome adversity. 兴趣有治愈情感创伤的力量，让我们能够克服困难。

empower *v*. 授权于；使更强大

adversity *n*. 困难，逆境

4. Without it, we cannot endure the trials, accomplish extraordinary

achievements, or revel in our accomplishments. 没有它，我们就不能忍受考验，无法取得非凡的成就，也不能享受自己的成就。（通过“endure ..., accomplish ..., or revel in ...”三个并列的谓语来加强语气）

revel *v.* 陶醉；狂欢作乐

点评

本篇文章结构非常清晰：第一段，引入话题，表明主旨观点；第二至第四段，阐述选择“个人兴趣”作为考虑因素的三个理由，每一个层次都有主题句；第五段，简单阐述为什么不选其他两个因素的原因；第六段，总结。

六、格言、谚语类作文

（一）范文示例①

2005 年上海高考作文

古人云：“天生我材必有用。(There must be a use for my talent.)”通过描述你生活中的一件事，说明人各有所长，无论才能大小，都能成为有用的人。

As the old saying goes, “There must be a use for my talent.” From my perspective, the essence of this saying lies in that each individual is born with unique talents. By recognizing and fully utilizing our talents, we can contribute to society in our own unique way.

The story of my neighbour is a typical example, which lends support to the meaning of the saying.【主题句】Unlike many of his peers, he did not have the opportunity to attend college due to his humble background. However, he never complained about his circumstances. Instead, he developed a skill in

① “范文示例”部分的范文来自詹玲：《高考英语写作专项训练》，上海教育出版社，2010，第 28 页。选作范文时有改动。

crafting customized wooden furniture. In an era, when buying ready-made furniture was a privilege, he willingly used his expertise to create wardrobes and dressing tables for his neighbours.

Moreover, he generously made toys for us, naughty children, without seeking any money. Consequently, not only did he earn a livelihood to support his family but also he won esteem from the local community.

This story of my neighbour enlightens me to the profound significance of the age-old saying. I firmly believe that regardless of the type of talent one possesses, there is always a way to showcase it. The key to success lies in self-confidence. As long as you believe in the value of your talents, you are bound to achieve success eventually, one way or another.

好词好句：

1. The story of my neighbour is a typical example, which lends support to the meaning of the saying. 我邻居的故事就是一个典型的例子，它证实了这句谚语的意义。（这是一句主题句，运用了较为复杂的非限制性定语从句）

2. In an era, when buying ready-made furniture was a privilege, he willingly used his expertise to create wardrobes and dressing tables for his neighbours. 在那个购买预制件是奢侈品的时代，他慷慨地利用自己的专业知识为邻居制作衣柜和梳妆台。（运用了 when 引导的定语从句修饰 era）

expertise *n*. 专门技能；专门知识；专长

3. Consequently, not only did he earn a livelihood to support his family but also he won esteem from the local community. 因此，他不仅赚钱养家，而且还赢得了当地社区的尊重。（运用了 not only … but also …并列分句）

esteem *n*. 尊重，敬重

4. This story of my neighbour enlightens me to the profound significance of the age-old saying. 我邻居的这个故事让我明白了这句古老的谚语的深刻意义。

enlighten *v*. 启发，教化；阐明

profound *adj*. 深厚的；意义深远的

点评

本篇文章结构为：第一段，引入谚语+定义+意义；第二、第三段，通过举例法讲述一个故事说明这个谚语的内涵；第四段，通过这个故事给“我”的启发来总结全文。

(二) 实战演练

假如你是李华，你报名参加了学校组织的“我用英语说中国故事”的演讲赛。比赛要求每位选手从“塞翁失马，焉知非福”(A blessing in disguise.)和“拔苗助长”(To pull up the seedlings to help them grow.)这两个成语中任选一个完成一篇演讲稿。演讲稿须包含以下内容：

1. 说明你选择的成语及其意义；
2. 运用具体事例来说明该成语给你的启发和感悟。

Our distinguished judges and dear fellow students,

My name is Li Hua. Today, I feel very privileged to stand here and deliver a speech centering on this traditional Chinese saying —"A blessing in disguise." As we high school students all know, "A blessing in disguise" means that we can't determine whether a frustration met in life is a curse or a blessing. If people handle it properly and see it from a positive angle, the difficulty may turn out to be a treasure.

Stephen Hawking, a great scientist who was diagnosed with a debilitating disease, was no longer able to move when he reached his twenties. However, instead of giving up in desperation and disappointment, he chose to face life with courage and went on to accomplish so much. With an optimistic attitude, Hawking immersed himself in the mysteries of the universe, developing many theories that are well-known by people today. His disability became a badge of honor that lets us recognize his greatness.

Just like Hawking, we are meeting barriers and difficulties in life every day. As far as I'm concerned, miracles will never happen if we look at things negatively. So why not keep moving and forget past mistakes? Painful and regretful as they might be, if we combine them with strong faith and continuous effort, those scars will finally fade away. They will take on a brand new look and power that can exert a far-reaching and lasting influence on our bright futures.

"A blessing in disguise" is just like a lighthouse on the ocean, motivating us to turn towards the horizon. May everyone here be strong enough to forgive and stay on course to pursue their dreams.

Thank you for listening.

好词好句：

1. Today, I feel very privileged to stand here and deliver a speech centering on this traditional Chinese saying. 今天，我很荣幸地站在这里，围绕这句中国传统谚语发表演讲。

privileged *adj*. 享有特权的；特许的

2. Stephen Hawking, a great scientist who was diagnosed with a debilitating disease, was no longer able to move when he reached his twenties. 史蒂芬·霍金是一位伟大的科学家，他被诊断出患有一种衰弱性疾病，20 多岁时就再也不能活动了。（... a great scientist who ... 用定语从句做同位语修饰 scientist，来说明霍金的身份）

debilitating *adj*. 使人非常虚弱的

3. Painful and regretful as they might be, if we combine them with strong faith and continuous effort, those scars will finally fade away. 尽管感到痛苦和遗憾，但如果我们把它们与坚定的信念和持续的努力结合起来，这些伤疤最终就会消失。（使用了 as 引导让步状语从句时的部分倒装结构）

fade away 逐渐消失

4. "A blessing in disguise" is just like a lighthouse on the ocean, motivating us to turn towards the horizon. "塞翁失马，焉知非福"就像海洋上的灯塔，激励我们转向地平线。（motivating 非谓语结构充当伴随状语）

点评

此篇文章体裁为：演讲稿＋谚语＋选择说理，融合了多种元素。这篇文章结构非常清晰，逻辑连贯，并且有读者意识，在开头、第三段和第五段中加入了演讲元素。词汇句型也较为丰富。

第二节　应用文

一、建议信

(一) 范文示例[①]

2014 年上海高考作文

学校英语报正在酝酿改版，拟从现有的三个栏目（健康、娱乐、文化）中去除一个，并从三个备选栏目（时尚、职业规划、读者反馈）中挑选一个纳入该报。假设你是该校学生程飞，给校报编辑写一封电子邮件，表达你的观点。邮件须包括以下内容：

1. 你建议去除的栏目及去除的理由；
2. 你建议增加的栏目及增加的理由。

Dear Editor,

I am thrilled to hear that our school's English newspaper is undergoing a revision of its columns. I am writing to offer my thoughts on this matter.

As far as I am concerned, the column that should be eliminated from the newspaper must be Entertainment. There are two compelling reasons justifying my proposal. 【主题句】 The first reason is that an overemphasis on entertainment can distract students from their studies. Some students, who are

① “范文示例”部分的范文来自詹玲：《高考英语写作专项训练》，上海教育出版社，2010，第 58 页。选作范文时有改动。

crazy and irrational fans of some stars, will pay too much attention to collecting the news of the stars, consequently neglecting their major task. The second reason lies in that columns focusing on health and culture are far more beneficial to students. They not only encourage a healthy lifestyle but also broaden students' horizons and enrich their minds. These aspects are crucial to students' overall development and should, therefore, be retained in the newspaper.

As for the column to be added, I believe that Career Planning can be a valuable addition.【主题句】Career Planning helps students identify and pursue their passions and areas of expertise at an early stage. There is abundant evidence suggesting that the earlier you plan for your future career, the more likely you are to avoid turns and twists, which helps you to excel your peer students.

My suggestions reflect the opinions of the majority of my classmates. I would greatly appreciate it if you could consider my ideas. I am eagerly looking forward to seeing the newspaper's wise change.

Yours sincerely,

Cheng Fei

好词好句:

1. As far as I am concerned, the column that should be eliminated from the newspaper must be Entertainment. There are two compelling reasons justifying my proposal. 在我看来,应该从报纸上去除的栏目必须是娱乐栏目。有两个令人信服的理由证明我的建议合理。(使用了定语从句以及用 justifying 非谓语结构来修饰 reasons)

compelling *adj*. 令人信服的;引人入胜的;令人信服的

2. The first reason is that ... The second reason lies in that ... 第一个原因是……第二个原因在于……(通过列举来说明原因)

3. Some students, who are crazy and irrational fans of some stars, will pay too much attention to collecting the news of the stars, consequently neglecting their major task. 有些学生是一些明星的疯狂和非理性的粉丝,

他们会把太多的注意力放在收集明星的新闻上，从而忽视了他们的主要任务。（运用了一个 who 引导的非限制性定语从句和 neglecting 非谓语结构做结果状语）

irrational *adj*. 不合理的，荒谬的

4. There is abundant evidence suggesting that the earlier you plan for your future career, the more likely you are to avoid turns and twists, which helps you to excel your peer students. 有大量的证据表明，你对未来的职业生涯规划得越早，你就越有可能避免走弯路，这有助于你超越同龄人。（运用了 suggesting 非谓语结构、"the＋比较级，the＋比较级"的结构和 which 引导的非限制性定语从句）

点评

文章的基本结构：第一段，交代事由＋写信意图，开门见山；第二段，阐述了要去除的栏目以及两个理由（详写）；第三段，阐述了要加入的栏目以及理由（略写）；第四段，总结。

整篇文章要素齐全，内容完整，逻辑清晰，很好地使用了主题句，主体部分详略得当，词汇、句型非常丰富。值得一提的是，在第二段分析为什么要去掉 Entertainment 这一栏目时，作者不仅分析了该栏目为什么不适合，而且阐述了为什么要保留 Health 和 Culture 这两个栏目，体现了一定的思辨能力。这是一篇不可多得的优秀范文。

（二）实战演练

2017 年上海秋考作文

假设你是明启中学的王磊，你校学生会将组织一次徒步活动，并在校园网公布了如下方案，征求师生意见。写一封邮件给活动组织者，内容须包括：

1. 你认为方案中需要改进的地方及改进建议；

2. 你的理由。

活动方案
主题：发现上海 时间：5 月 1 日(星期日)下午 3:00 路线：从人民广场出发，途经南京东路，抵达外滩(the Bund)后原路返回

To whom it may concern,

We have received information that the student union is planning to organize a hiking activity within our city. It has been requested that both teachers and students provide their opinions on its organization. I am truly honored to express my personal perspective regarding this proposed event.

Firstly, as far as the theme—"To Discover Shanghai" is concerned, I think we had better change the route. 【主题句】Instead of retracing our steps, we should strive to incorporate as many prominent landmarks as possible into our route, enabling participants to fully appreciate Shanghai's rich historical heritage and iconic architectural marvels. For example, when we arrive at the Bund, we can walk along the Bund, appreciating the magnificent architectural wonders there, and then pay a visit to the Yu Garden. Only in this way, can we adhere closely to this designated theme.

Secondly, I hold reservations concerning the chosen date. 【主题句】On Sunday, May 1st, Nanjing Road is likely to be congested with tourists and pedestrians, which can prove harmful to the overall success of our event. In light of this, I propose that we schedule the hiking activity on a workday, thus to avoid the unnecessary overcrowding.

I earnestly hope that you will take my suggestion into careful consideration. I genuinely wish for the event to achieve resounding success.

Yours sincerely,

Wang Lei

好词好句：

1. Instead of retracing our steps, we should strive to incorporate as many prominent landmarks as possible into our route, enabling participants to fully

appreciate Shanghai's rich historical heritage and iconic architectural marvels. 我们不应该走回路，而应该努力将尽可能多的著名地标融入我们的路线，让参与者充分欣赏上海丰富的历史遗产和标志性的建筑奇迹。（运用 enabling 非谓语结构充当伴随状语）

incorporate *v*. 组成公司；包含；混合　*adj*. 合并的

heritage *n*. 遗产；传统

iconic *adj*. 符号的；图标的

2. Only in this way, can we adhere closely to this designated theme. 只有这样，我们才能紧密地坚持这个指定的主题。（Only＋介词短语位于句首引起的部分倒装）

3. On Sunday, May 1st, Nanjing Road is likely to be congested with tourists and pedestrians, which can prove harmful to the overall success of our event. 在5月1日星期日这天，南京路很可能会挤满游客和行人，这可能会对我们活动的整体成功造成影响。（运用了 which 引导的非限制性定语从句）

4. In light of this, I propose that we schedule the hiking activity on a workday, thus to avoid the unnecessary overcrowding. 鉴于此，我建议把徒步活动安排在工作日，从而避免不必要的拥挤。（运用了 propose that 结构；to avoid 非谓语结构充当目的状语）

点评

该作文题是2017年的上海秋考作文真题，要求学生在以“发现上海”为主题的一次徒步活动的方案中发现问题，提出解决方案并阐述理由。不仅考查了学生的语言能力，还考查了学生的思维品质，如发现问题、分析问题、解决问题的能力。如果学生能提出创新性的解决方案，则有可能得到高分。这个作文题考查了多个维度的英语学科核心素养，是一道非常不错的作文题。

本文第一段，交代了写信的事由以及写信的意图。第二段从主题“发现上海”出发，指出路线上存在的问题，并给出了具体的理由和解决方案。第三段从时间出发，指出存在的问题，并给出具体的理由和解决方案。该篇文章非常切题，学生非常善于发现问题并能给出合理的解决方案。语言丰富且多变，是一篇难得的佳作。

二、申请信

(一) 范文示例

2011 年上海高考作文

若你是明启中学李明，想申请一个扶贫项目，帮助贫困地区的儿童。根据以下启事写一封申请信(信中不能提到真实的姓名和学校)。

启事：

国际儿童基金会将资助中学生开展扶贫项目，以帮助贫困地区的儿童。申请成功者将获得项目经费 2 000 元。有意者请来信告知。

信中请包括：

1. 你个人的基本情况；2. 你对申请项目的具体设想；3. 项目经费使用情况。

Dear Sir/Madam,

I am Li Ming, a student from Shanghai. I am writing to you today to request a grant of 2,000 yuan to support a project I have designed to assist children in the poverty-stricken areas.

Having grown up in an urban environment, I have never personally experienced the hardships faced by my peers in poor regions. However, I firmly hold the view that the true value of our lives lies in the extent to which we lend a helping hand to those who need it. As a result, I have been actively involved in charitable efforts and have gained valuable experience in organizing such projects.

My poverty-relief project has a carefully crafted plan. 【主题句】 Firstly, I plan to purchase textbooks and also gather literature books from my friends. Additionally, I plan to recruit top-rated students as volunteers, who will aid struggling students in overcoming learning difficulties. Along with the books and volunteers, we will visit pre-selected schools that are in need of assistance.

When it comes to allocation of funds, I propose to divide one-third for purchasing books and two-thirds to cover the travel expenses of the volunteers.

I would greatly appreciate it if you could consider and approve my funding request. I am eagerly anticipating your response.

Yours sincerely,

Li Ming

好词好句：

1. Having grown up in an urban environment, I have never personally experienced the hardships faced by my peers in poor regions. 我在城市环境中长大，从未经历过贫困地区的同龄人所面临的困难。（使用了动名词结构做主语）

2. However, I firmly hold the view that the true value of our lives lies in the extent to which we lend a helping hand to those who need it. 然而，我坚信，我们生命的真正价值在于我们帮助那些需要帮助的人的程度。

3. Additionally, I plan to recruit top-rated students as volunteers, who will aid struggling students in overcoming learning difficulties. 此外，我计划招募成绩最好的学生作为志愿者，他们将帮助有困难的学生克服学习困难。（使用了 who 引导的非限制性定语从句）

4. When it comes to allocation of funds, I propose to divide one-third for purchasing books and two-thirds to cover the travel expenses of the volunteers. 至于资金的分配，我建议将三分之一用于购买书籍，三分之二用于支付志愿者的差旅费用。

when it comes to 谈到；涉及

点评

本文是 2011 年的高考作文，文章为典型的“五段式”结构。第一段，交代事由＋写信目的；第二段，介绍个人的基本情况；第三段，对申请项目的具体设想；第四段，项目经费使用情况；第五段，总结。

文章要点齐全，内容翔实，通过使用主题句、多变的句型和丰富的词汇，体现了作者较高的英语学科核心素养。

(二) 实战演练

假设你是一名高一学生。这个暑假，学校将会迎来一批来沪交流的英国学生，你打算申请作为志愿者参加这次学生交流项目，写一封申请信给学校负责人。

信中请包括：

1. 你个人的基本情况；
2. 申请的理由；
3. 有哪些活动建议。

To whom it may concern,

Hearing that a group of British exchange students are coming to our school, I am very thrilled. Hardly can I wait to write to express my keen interest in volunteering for this exchange program.

First, please allow me to provide you with some details about myself.【主题句】I am currently a diligent and motivated student in Senior One, with a strong passion for cross-cultural exchange and language learning. I have actively participated in various extracurricular activities, including public speaking and debate clubs, which have improved my communication skills. Moreover, my proficiency in English will enable me to effectively engage with the British students and assist them in their cultural immersion.

I have every reason to justify my application.【主题句】The main reason for my application lies in the desire to broaden my perspectives through firsthand experiences with international students. By interacting with British students, I can gain a better understanding of their culture and traditions. With globalization continuing to shape our world, it is crucial for me to develop a global mindset and embrace diversity. This exchange program provides an exceptional platform for such growth. To plus, it is also a golden opportunity to enhance my language abilities.

In terms of suggestions, I propose we should conduct orientation sessions before the British students arrive to familiarize the volunteers with their respective roles and responsibilities. This can ensure that we are well-prepared to provide the necessary support and assistance during their stay. Furthermore, organizing cultural excursions or trips to local attractions can allow the visiting students to experience the diverse heritage and lifestyles of our city.

Thank you for considering my application to become a volunteer for this student exchange program. Please do not hesitate to contact me. And I sincerely wish the event a great success.

Yours sincerely,

Li Ming

好词好句:

1. I have actively participated in various extracurricular activities, including public speaking and debate clubs, which have improved my communication skills. 我积极参加各种课外活动,包括公开演讲和辩论俱乐部,这提高了我的沟通能力。(运用了 which 引导的非限制性定语从句)

extracurricular *adj*. 学校课程以外的

2. With globalization continuing to shape our world, it is crucial for me to develop a global mindset and embrace diversity. 随着全球化继续塑造我们的世界,发展全球心态和拥抱多样性对我来说至关重要。(运用了 with 的宾语补足语结构和 it 引导的句型)

mindset *n*. 观念模式,思维倾向

embrace *v*. 拥抱;欣然接受　*n*. 拥抱;接受,信奉

3. Furthermore, organizing cultural excursions or trips to local attractions can allow the visiting students to experience the diverse heritage and lifestyles of our city. 此外,组织文化游览或到当地景点旅游,可以让访问学生体验我们城市多样的遗产和生活方式。(运用了 organizing 动名词结构充当主语)

diverse heritage 多样的遗产

4. Please do not hesitate to contact me. And I sincerely wish the event a

great success. 请随时与我联系。我真诚地祝愿这次活动取得圆满成功。(文章的结尾部分,作者对读者说如果觉得申请合乎要求的话,请联系他/她,并预祝活动成功,体现了读者意识)

点评

本篇作文的话题取自我校的一次真实活动,年级内有不少学生即将参加这次志愿者活动。本文第一段,开门见山地交代了事由和写信意图。第二至第四段分别交代了个人情况、申请理由以及活动建议。值得一提的是,在该生的活动建议中,提到了应该先对志愿者们进行一定的指导这一比较有创意的想法,体现了一定的创新性思维同时又非常合情合理。本篇文章语言丰富多变,是篇不错的范文。

三、演讲稿

(一) 范文示例①

请写一篇演讲稿,代表同学们在毕业前的最后一次班会上表达对老师的感激之情。

Good morning, everyone,

This is the last class meeting. Thinking that we are to graduate and leave the teachers who have accompanied us for three years, I have a mixed feeling of excitement, sadness and the most important, gratitude. Now, on behalf of all my classmates, I want to say to our dearest teachers, "Thank you from the very bottom of our heart."

During the three years, it is you who enlighten our mind and expand our horizons, making us equipped with the knowledge necessary for further

① "范文示例"部分的作文题目及范文来自詹玲:《高考英语写作专项训练》,上海教育出版社,2010,第 54—55 页。选作范文时有改动。

studies. It is you who tap our creative potential and help us to be independent learners. It is you who tell us the importance of being honest, understanding and generous. And you practise what you preach. You remind us to look at the world objectively in order to make sensible judgement each time we encounter adversities. You devote yourselves to helping us without asking for anything in return. Without your guidance, help and enlightenment, we wouldn't have grown up and become ambitious, determined and brave.

Thank you, our dear teachers. We owe our growth to you. You have done your part to cultivate us and now it is our turn to do something in return. Your efforts are bound to pay off.

So much for my speech. Thank you for listening!

好词好句：

1. Thinking that we are to graduate and leave the teachers who have accompanied us for three years, I feel a mixed feeling of excitement, sadness and the most important, gratitude. 一想到我们就要毕业了，要离开陪伴了我们三年的老师，我有一种兴奋、悲伤，最重要的是感激的复杂心情。（此句运用了-ing的分词结构和定语从句）

2. During the three years, it is you who enlighten our mind and expand our horizons, making us equipped with the knowledge necessary for further studies. 在这三年里，是你们启发了我们的思想，拓宽了我们的视野，为我们提供了进一步学习所需要的知识。（此句运用了 it 引导的强调句型和 making 非谓语结构充当伴随状语）

enlighten *v.* 启发，教化；阐明

3. We owe our growth to you. You have done your part to cultivate us and now it is our turn to do something in return. 我们的成长归功于你们。你们已经尽了你们的一份力来培养我们，现在轮到我们做些回报了。

owe A to B 把 A 归功于 B

4. Your efforts are bound to pay off. 你的努力一定会得到回报的。

be bound to 很有可能，肯定会

pay off 取得成功，有回报

点评

第一段，引出演讲的主题；第二段，通过一系列的强调句型构成排比，阐述老师对学生无微不至的帮助和关怀；第三段，表达对老师深深的谢意；第四段，演讲收尾，感谢垂听。

整篇文章结构清晰，逻辑严谨。同时，文章词汇丰富，表达多样化，对老师的感激情深意切，是一篇非常不错的演讲稿。

（二）实战演练

班级将进行一场以“My Dream”为题的演讲比赛，写一篇英文演讲稿，须包含以下内容：

1. 简单介绍你的梦想；
2. 阐述理由；
3. 如何实现你的梦想。

Hi,

Good afternoon! It's an honor to stand here today to share with you my dream and the reasons behind it. First and foremost, my dream is to become an environmentalist. I have always been passionate about protecting our planet and ensuring its sustainability for future generations. The deteriorating state of our environment has motivated me to take action.

There are several reasons why I am so drawn to this field.【主题句】Firstly, I believe that by preserving our planet's natural resources and ecosystems, we can create a better world for everyone. Climate change, pollution, and deforestation are all critical issues that need immediate attention and solutions. Secondly, I am inspired by individuals who have dedicated their lives to environmental conservation and have witnessed the positive impact of their efforts. Their stories have ignited a fire within me to contribute in my own way.

To achieve my dream, I plan to pursue a degree in environmental science and gain practical experience through internships and volunteer work.【主题句】By studying this subject, I will acquire the necessary knowledge and skills to tackle environmental challenges. Additionally, I aim to raise awareness about environmental issues among my peers and community through organizing workshops, campaigns, and creating online content. It is important to me that everyone understands the urgency and the role they can play in protecting our environment.

In conclusion, my dream of becoming an environmentalist is fueled by my deep concern for the planet and the desire to make a positive impact. I believe that wit· knowledge, dedication, and collective efforts, we can create a more sustainable future. Let's join hands and work towards a greener and cleaner world for ourselves and generations to come.

Thank you for listening!

好词好句：

1. The deteriorating state of our environment has motivated me to take action. 不断恶化的环境促使我采取行动。

deteriorating *adj*. 不断变坏的

2. Secondly, I am inspired by individuals who have dedicated their lives to environmental conservation and have witnessed the positive impact of their efforts. 第二，我被那些毕生致力于环境保护的人所鼓舞并目睹了他们的努力产生的积极影响。(运用了 who 引导的定语从句)

3. Their stories have ignited a fire within me to contribute in my own way. 他们的故事在我内心点燃了火焰，让我以自己的方式做贡献。

ignite *v*. 点燃

点评

本篇演讲稿结构：第一段，引入演讲主题，简单介绍梦想；第二段，阐述理由；第三段，实现理想的方法；第四、第五段：总结并感谢观众垂听。整篇演讲结构严谨，思路清晰。词汇丰富多变。

四、倡议书

(一) 范文示例

假设你是明启中学的高三学生李华。你校最近请你围绕“创建美好的校园环境”这一主题，用英语给全校同学写一封倡议书。内容如下：

1. 不要乱扔垃圾，要爱护花草树木；
2. 不得高声喧哗；
3. 循环使用材料；
4. 保持教室整洁。

Dear fellow students,

As a Senior Three student, I am here today to appeal to all of you to create a better school environment. Our school is our second home, a place where we grow, learn, and socialize. It is essential to maintain a clean, peaceful, and sustainable campus for the benefit and well-being of everyone.

To achieve this, I propose the following actions and requirements for all students.

Firstly, stop littering.【主题句】Let's show respect for our school by properly disposing of trash. Use designated bins for different types of waste and encourage others to do the same. Together, we can keep our campus free from litter and protect our beautiful flowers, plants, and trees.

Secondly, maintain quiet surroundings.【主题句】Let's be mindful of our noise levels. Avoid shouting or making loud noises that disturb the learning environment. By maintaining a peaceful atmosphere, we can concentrate better and show consideration for our classmates.

Thirdly, practice recycling.【主题句】Let's actively engage in recycling efforts. Use reusable water bottles, recycle paper and plastic waste, and support initiatives that promote the reduction of waste. Through responsible consumption and recycling, we can minimize our ecological footprint.

Fourthly, keep classrooms tidy. 【主题句】Let's take responsibility for keeping our classrooms clean and organized. Clean up after ourselves, arrange desks and chairs properly, and take care of the school supplies. Only by maintaining a clean learning environment can we create a conducive space for effective studying and teamwork.

Together, we have the power to bring about positive change. I firmly believe that by embracing these simple yet important actions, we can create a welcoming and harmonious campus for all. Let us join hands towards a better future for our school and ourselves. Thank you for your attention and support.

好词好句：

1. It is essential to maintain a clean, peaceful, and sustainable campus for the benefit and well-being of everyone. 为了每个人的利益和福祉，必须保持一个干净、和平和可持续的校园。（运用了 it 做形式主语的不定式结构）

sustainable *adj*. 可持续的

2. Let's show respect for our school by properly disposing of trash. 让我们通过妥善处理垃圾来表示对学校的尊重。

dispose of 丢掉；处理

3. Use designated bins for different types of waste and encourage others to do the same. 使用指定的垃圾箱存放不同类型的垃圾，并鼓励其他人也这样做。

designated *adj*. 指定的

4. Let's be mindful of our noise levels. 让我们注意一下我们的噪声水平。

5. Through responsible consumption and recycling, we can minimize our ecological footprint. 通过负责任的消费和回收利用，我们可以最大限度地减少我们的生态足迹。

6. Only by maintaining a clean learning environment can we create a conducive space for effective studying and teamwork. 只有保持一个干净的学习环境，我们才能为有效的学习和团队合作创造一个有利的空间。（运用了Only＋介词短语位于句首引起的部分倒装结构）

点评

本篇文章的基本结构为：第一段，发起倡议的事由和目的；第二至六段，所倡议的具体要求和内容；第七段，倡议者的信心和呼吁。

文章结构清晰，要点齐全，内容翔实。

(二) 实战演练

随着生活条件的不断改善，越来越多的人喜欢出游度假，但遗憾的是一些游客的不文明行为屡见不鲜。请你给全校同学写一封关于文明出游的倡议书。内容须包括：

1. 你对这种现象的看法；
2. 提出倡议。

Dear fellow students,

With the improvement of people's living conditions, an increasing number of people choose to go on vacation whenever possible. But it is a pity that cases where some tourists spit, litter, scribble, make loud noises, jump the queue in tourist destinations are often seen, which brings about some consequences worse than we have imagined. So today I am writing to appeal to all of you to take action to fight against the bad phenomena.【倡议书的目的】

When we travel to other cities, these uncivilized habits will destroy the beauty and harmony of the places, and even worse, damage the relics or disturb the balance of ecosystem, causing great trouble to local people. What's more, if we travel abroad, our improper behavior may leave a bad impression on the locals and gradually we will gain a notorious reputation for being ill-mannered, leading to a very negative national image.

Consequently, I appeal to every student to raise our civilization consciousness and be a self-disciplined tourist.【主题句】When visiting resorts, we should throw rubbish into the dustbin and always keep garbage classification in mind. Don't make noises in public and don't spit. Do wait in a line patiently and be sure not to scrawl. At the same time, show our respect for local customs and tradition, and it is better not to disturb the normal life of locals.

There is no denying that travelling not only does good to people's mental and physical health but also is financially beneficial to local economy. However, only when we behave ourselves well can we really benefit from tourism. So, let's take action immediately and ask our friends, relatives to join us to create a harmonious society and sustainable tourism. Thanks for your attention!

好词好句：

1. But it is a pity that cases where some tourists spit, litter, scribble, make loud noises, jump the queue in tourist destinations are often seen, which brings about some consequences worse than we have imagined. 但遗憾的是，在旅游目的地经常看到游客吐痰、乱扔垃圾、乱涂乱画、大声喧哗、插队的情况，造成的后果比我们想象的还要糟。（运用了 which 引导的非限制性定语从句）

2. When we travel to other cities, these uncivilized habits will destroy the beauty and harmony of the places, and even worse, damage the relics or disturb the balance of ecosystem, causing great trouble to local people. 当我们去其他城市旅游时，这些不文明的习惯会破坏当地的美丽与和谐，更糟糕的是，破坏文物或扰乱生态系统的平衡，会给当地人带来很大的麻烦。（运用了 causing 非谓语结构充当伴随状语）

3. However, only when we behave ourselves well can we really benefit from tourism. 然而，只有当我们表现良好时，我们才能真正从旅游业中受益。（运用了 only 修饰状语从句位于句首引起的部分倒装）

点评

本文的第一段，通过简述旅游中存在不文明行为的现象，引出此封倡议书的目的。第二段为旅游中不文明的行为带来的严重后果，即为什么要进行倡议的原因。第三段通过一个主题句引出我们在旅游中应该做什么、不应该做什么，内容非常翔实。最后一段通过呼吁号召总结全文。文章结构清晰，语言丰富多变，是一篇不错的范文。

第三节 记叙文

一、叙事言情类作文

(一) 范文示例

2009 年北京高考作文

假设你是红星中学高三一班的学生李华，为响应绿化祖国的号召，你班 4 月 12 日去郊区植树，请根据以下四幅图的先后顺序，介绍植树活动的全过程，给某英文杂志的“绿色行动”专栏写一篇“Green Action in Our Class”为题的英文稿件。（注意：词数不少于 60。提示词：郊区 suburbs）

Green Action in Our Class

April 12 will forever remain in our memories as a remarkable day when our class participated in a significant endeavor, leaving a profound impact on us.

In the early morning, we cheerfully rode our bicycles to the outskirts to plant trees, engaging in lively chatter and hearty laughter throughout the trip. Despite the biting cold, none of us uttered a single complaint. Upon our arrival, we promptly got to work without delay. Everyone took part actively: some carried and planted the saplings, others dug the ground diligently, while a few attentively watered the trees. In no time did rows of trees appear, filling us with a sense of fulfillment.

Before leaving, we put up a signboard, reading "Nurture nature", which reminded passersby to contribute to environmental protection.

At the sight of those young trees, a wave of relief washed over us, coupled with a sense of achievement. We profoundly realized that if everyone made a small contribution to protecting the environment, we would be able to foster a more vibrant city and an improved quality of life.

好词好句：

1. April 12 will forever remain in our memories as a remarkable day when our class participated in a significant endeavor, leaving a profound impact on us. 4 月 12 日将永远留在我们的记忆中，这是一个非凡的日子，我们班付出了很大的努力，对我们产生了深远的影响。（运用了 leaving 非谓语结构充当伴随状语）

profound *adj*. 深刻的；意义深远的；严重的

2. In the early morning, we cheerfully rode our bicycles to the outskirts to plant trees, engaging in lively chatter and hearty laughter throughout the trip. 清晨，我们高高兴兴地骑车去郊外植树，一路上谈笑风生。（运用了 engaging 非谓语结构充当伴随状语）

the outskirts 郊外

3. Everyone took part actively: some carried and planted the saplings,

others dug the ground diligently, while a few attentively watered the trees. In no time did rows of trees appear, filling us with a sense of fulfillment. 每个人都积极地参与：有的人运输和种植树苗，有的人勤奋地挖地，还有一些人聚精会神地给树木浇水。不一会儿，一排排的树木映入眼帘，让我们充满了成就感。（本句通过一个简单句总起，后接一个主从复合句来说明情况，最后再通过一个句子总结）

sapling *n.* 幼树，树苗

4. At the sight of those young trees, a wave of relief washed over us, coupled with a sense of achievement. 看到那些小树，我们如释重负，同时也有一种成就感。（在主句前后各运用了 seeing 和 coupled 非谓语结构做状语）

点评

文章第一段，总起，引入事件；第二、第三段，以时间为顺序生动阐述事件的整个过程；第四段，通过该事件表达自己的观点和抒发自己的感情。

整篇文章为总—分—总结构，事件以时间顺序展开，思路清晰，语言丰富生动，起到了很好的叙事言情效果。

（二）实战演练

在你的人生中，一定经历过很多难以忘怀的时刻，请以“An Unforgettable Moment”为题，写一篇文章，内容必须包含以下要点：

1. 描述这个时刻；
2. 谈谈你的感受和它对你的影响。

An Unforgettable Moment

Gone are the days when I was a kid, playing without concerns and worries, but that day still remains fresh in my memory.

It was a hot summer evening when I was playing cheerfully with friends in the park. But our game was abruptly interrupted by an old man, who was approaching us slowly without a word. He made an attempt to communicate with us with gestures. I was suddenly aware that he might be deaf. So afraid was I that I burst into tears and ran away, thinking that he was weird. However, I couldn't forget his sad and ashamed face until now. 【具体事件描述】

Years later, recalling that moment, I still can't help feeling regretful. 【主题句】As an adult, I have realized the serious hurt I had brought to that old man on that evening. There shouldn't be any prejudice against the people with disabilities and what our ordinary people should offer to them is respect, love and care.

Since then, I have realized everyone has the right to be treated equally. Immersed in social endeavors, I have sought to extend a healing hand to those challenged by adversity, bridging the gaps that divide us, to make up for that innocent mistake. I hope with more people participating, our world can become more beautiful.

好词好句：

1. Gone are the days when I was a kid, playing without concerns and worries, but that day still remains fresh in my memory. 当我还是个孩子的时候，无忧无虑玩耍的日子已经一去不复返了，但那一天我仍然记忆犹新。（运用了 gone are the days when ...的特殊句型和 playing 非谓语结构）

2. But our game was abruptly interrupted by an old man, who was approaching us slowly without a word. 但是我们的游戏突然被一个老人打断了，他一句话也没有说，慢慢地向我们靠近。（运用了 who 引导的非限制性定语从句）

abruptly *adv*. 突然地；意外地；（言谈举止）唐突地

3. So afraid was I that I burst into tears and ran away, thinking that he was weird. 我太害怕了，哭着跑开了，觉得他很奇怪。（运用了 so 引导的倒装结构和 thinking 非谓语结构）

4. Immersed in social endeavors, I have sought to extend a healing hand to those challenged by adversity, bridging the gaps that divide us, to make up for that innocent mistake. 沉浸在社会活动中，我试图向那些被逆境挑战的人伸出治愈的手，弥合我们之间的鸿沟，以弥补那个无知的错误。（运用了 immersed 和 bridging 非谓语结构，整个句子结构比较复杂）

immersed *adj*. 浸入的，沉入的

点评

第一段，引入话题；第二段，具体描述该事件；第三段，谈自己的遗憾和感受；第四段，这件事情对自己的影响。

作者通过首段的引入，中间段主题句的合理使用，使得文章思路清晰，结构严谨。在词汇和句型方面，多处使用了从句和非谓语结构，词汇也非常丰富生动，是一篇非常不错的叙事言情类文章。

二、写人、状物类作文

（一）范文示例①

改编自 2008 年湖南高考作文

请从下列人物中选择你最喜欢的一位，用英语写一篇短文。文章须包含以下内容：

1. 对该人物的简单介绍；
2. 喜欢该人物的理由；
3. 该人物对你的影响。

Tomas Edison	Helen Keller	William Shakespeare
inventor; creative; diligent; full of wisdom	ordinary but great woman; disabled; optimistic; eager to learn	writer; talented; imaginative; man of all ages
"Genius is one percent inspiration and ninety-nine percent perspiration."	"... if I had the power of sight for three days."	"Life is a stage ..."

① "范文示例"部分的范文来自詹玲：《高考英语写作专项训练》，上海教育出版社，2010，第 39—40 页。选作范文时有改动。

My favourite person among the three is, without any doubt, Helen Keller, an ordinary but great woman. She lost her sight and hearing when she was only three in an accident. But she got over lots of unimaginable adversities to learn languages and ultimately she mastered 8 different languages and wrote a wealth of books.

I like Helen Keller for numerous reasons, especially her optimism and perseverance. 【主题句】Handicapped though she was, she didn't lose hope for life. Instead, she was eager to learn. Just imagine how a little girl who couldn't see or hear learned to read and write!

Despite all these adversities, she didn't give up halfway. 【主题句】Her books are the best proof of her unrelenting efforts. Throughout her life, she completed 14 books, among which *Three Days to See* is the most famous.

The story of Helen has a profound influence on me. 【主题句】Everytime I want to give up on account of the failure or frustration, the image of Helen will flash into my mind. I seem to hear her saying, "A little more effort, and you will achieve your goal." Inspired by Helen Keller, I come to realize the essence of the saying, "Nothing is impossible for a person with persistence."

好词好句：

1. Despite all these adversities, she didn't give up halfway. 尽管有这些逆境，但她并没有半途而废。

2. Her books are the best proof of her unrelenting efforts. 她的书是她不懈努力的最好证明。

unrelenting *adj*. 无情的；不松懈的；不屈不挠的

3. Throughout her life, she completed 14 books, among which *Three Days to See* is the most famous. 在她的一生中，完成了14本书，其中《假如给我三天光明》一书是最著名的。(运用了which引导的非限制性定语从句)

4. I seem to hear her saying, "A little more effort, and you will achieve your goal."我似乎听到她说："再多努力一点，你就会实现你的目标。"(本句引用了海伦·凯勒的一句名言来说明她对自己的影响)

5. Inspired by Helen Keller, I come to realize the essence of the saying,

"Nothing is impossible for a person with perseverance." 受到海伦·凯勒的启发，我开始认识到这句话的本质："对于一个有毅力的人来说，没有什么是不可能的。"（运用了 inspired 非谓语结构，最后通过引用一句谚语来结束全文并点题）

点评

文章结构：第一段，引入主题，简单介绍人物事迹；第二、第三段，对应题目要求，阐述喜欢该人物的理由；第四段，阐述该人物对自己的影响并通过谚语来总结全文。

本篇文章通过合理使用主题句，使得结构非常清晰，并很好地对应了题目的要求。词汇丰富，句型多变。尾段通过引用海伦·凯勒的名言以及一句谚语来总结全文，起到了卒章显志的作用，是一篇记人言情的佳作。

（二）实战演练

My Favourite ________

1. 描述你最喜欢的一本书、一部电影或一个人；
2. 说明你对其印象深刻的理由。

I have read a wealth of books. But if asked which is my favourite, I will say *The old man and the sea* by Hemingway without hesitation.

It's about a white-haired aged man who lives by fishing in the sea all the year around.【主题句】After 84 fruitless days on the sea, he finally catches a big fish, bigger than his boat. Unfortunately, groups of sharks are attracted. In the process of fighting with the sharks, the meat of the big fish is eaten up by the sharks. As a result, what the old man get is just a skeleton of the big fish. It is the old man's fighting with the sharks that impresses me most in the whole novel, which can be justified by two reasons.

In the first place, it is the words of Hemingway that impresses me so much.【主题句】Using simple but powerful words, Hemingway can always use the most concise words to convey his ideas to his readers so directly and precisely. Besides, Hemingway is a genius to visualize his story by his vivid language. When I am reading the scene, I can feel as if the old man were fighting with the sharks in front of me, which really stuns me.

To plus, it is the spirit of the scene that inspires me most. 【主题句】 Before that moment, the old man has gone through 84 fruitless days and two days of fierce fight with the fish. But this time, what he is faced with is the danger from the sharks. However, again, he chooses to face up to the difficulty. While what he finally gets is just a skeleton of the big fish, the bravery and perseverance makes him a true hero. As Hemingway says in the book, a man can be destroyed but not defeated. The old man makes it.

There's no denying that *The Old Man and the Sea* is an enduring classic and I will keep in mind the fighting moment of the old man, for it can inspire me to go through the ups and downs in my whole life.

好词好句：

1. I have read a wealth of books. But if asked which is my favourite, I will say *The Old Man and the Sea* by Hemingway without hesitation. 我读了很多书。但如果问我最喜欢哪一本，我会毫不犹豫地说是海明威的《老人与海》。（运用了 asked 非谓语结构）

2. It is the old man's fighting with the sharks that impresses me most in the whole novel, which can be justified by two reasons. 在整部小说中，给我印象最深刻的是老人与鲨鱼的搏斗，有两个理由。（运用了 it 强调句型和 which 引导的非限制性定语从句）

3. When I am reading the scene, I can feel as if the old man were fighting with the sharks in front of me, which really stuns me. 当我读到这个场景时，我能感觉到老人和鲨鱼在我面前搏斗，这真的让我很震惊。（运用了 as if 的虚拟语气和 which 引导的非限制性定语从句）

stun *v.* 使目瞪口呆；击晕，使昏厥；使震聋

4. There's no denying that *The Old Man and the Sea* is an enduring classic and I will keep in mind the fighting moment of the old man, for it can inspire me to go through the ups and downs in my whole life. 不可否认，《老人

与海》是一部经久不衰的经典作品，我会记住老人的搏斗时刻，因为它可以激励我走过人生的起起伏伏。（运用了 there is no denying that ...的特殊句型）

enduring *adj*. 持久的，不朽的

点评

第一段，引入话题；第二段，简要描述该书的内容；第三、第四段，阐述喜欢这本书的理由；第五段，总结。

整篇文章结构清晰，采用了总—分—总的结构。对于故事的描述非常生动，对于喜欢的理由从文字和精神两方面进行了阐述，层层递进。文章语言丰富，变化多样，是一篇不可多得的学生佳作。

主要参考文献

[1] 甘兰.美国大学英语写作[M].6 版.北京：外语教学与研究出版社，2007.

[2] 何亚男，金怡，张育青，等.高中英语写作教学设计[M].上海：上海教育出版社，2017.

[3] 何亚男，应晓球.落实学科核心素养在课堂[M].上海：上海教育出版社，2021.

[4] 李蒨，王宏年，汤青.激活语言思维：高中英语写作教学指南[M].南京：江苏凤凰科学技术出版社，2016.

[5] 罗伯特・J. 马扎诺，黛布拉・皮克林，塔米・赫夫尔鲍尔.高度参与的课堂：提高学生专注力的沉浸式教学[M].白洁，译.北京：中国青年出版社，2019.

[6] 詹玲.高考英语写作专项训练[M].上海：上海教育出版社，2011.

[7] 中华人民共和国教育部.普通高中英语课程标准(2017 年版 2020 年修订)[S].北京：人民教育出版社，2020.

[8] Brookes A., Grundy P. Beginning to write[M]. Cambridge: Cambridge University Press, 1999.

[9] Evans V. Successful writing[M]. London: Express Publishing, 2000.

[10] Krich G., Roen D. H. A sense of audience in written communication[M]. Newbury Park: Sage, 1990.

[11] Zemach D. E., Rumisek L. A. Academic writing: From paragragh to essay[M]. London: Macmillan Education, 2005.

后　记

在高中英语教学中，英语写作占据了极其重要的地位。为了帮助学生提高英语写作水平，同时也为了帮助教师更好地开展写作教学，我编写了这本《核心素养下高中英语写作的教与学》。编写这本书的初衷源于我对高中英语写作教学中的一些困惑和挑战。我发现，学生在审题、谋篇布局、段落处理、句型结构等写作方面存在一些困难，而教师在教学过程中也面临着如何激发学生兴趣、指导学生思考和创作、提供具体的指导和反馈等问题。因此，我希望通过这本书，为学生和教师提供一些有价值的指导和建议，使他们能够更好地掌握英语写作的技巧，提升写作水平。

在编写此书的过程中，我遇到了不少挑战。首先是如何将抽象的写作理论转化为实用的写作技巧。我通过列举具体的例子和进行实践操作，结合各种学生实际可用的工具，如评价量表、思维导图等，让学生能够更有效地理解并内化理论知识，从而掌握实用的写作技巧并运用到写作中。其次是如何系统地整理和呈现写作教学的方法和技巧。书中尽可能涵盖写作的方方面面，并以简明易懂的方式呈现给读者，使他们能够更好地理解和运用。

在此，我要感谢所有对本书做出贡献的人。首先，我要感谢一直以来支持和帮助我的川沙中学校长王珏老师，正是她不断的督促和鼓励，让我有了编写这本书的勇气。其次，我要感谢我的基地导师——上海市建平中学教研组长吴文涛老师，她在我平时教学和教研工作方面给予了方方面面的指导，也对本书提出了很多宝贵的建议。再次，我还要感谢我们川沙中学英语组的老师们，他们在平时的教学工作中给了我莫大的帮助，并在一些教学实

践和案例写作方面给了我很多具体而有效的建议。最后，我也要感谢所有参与写作实践的学生，正是因为有他们的努力和实践，才有了本书丰富的素材和案例。

因本人能力所限，书中恐有谬误，欢迎广大读者批评指正。

童莉玲

2024年4月23日

图书在版编目(CIP)数据

核心素养下高中英语写作的教与学 / 童莉玲著. —
上海：上海教育出版社，2024.5
ISBN 978 - 7 - 5720 - 2673 - 7

Ⅰ.①核… Ⅱ.①童… Ⅲ.①英语课-教学研究-高
中 Ⅳ.①G633.412

中国国家版本馆 CIP 数据核字(2024)第 107993 号

责任编辑　方文琳　李　祥
封面设计　周　吉

核心素养下高中英语写作的教与学
童莉玲 著

出版发行　上海教育出版社有限公司
官　　网　www.seph.com.cn
地　　址　上海市闵行区号景路 159 弄 C 座
邮　　编　201101
印　　刷　上海颛辉印刷厂有限公司
开　　本　700×1000　1/16　印张 12.5
字　　数　204 千字
版　　次　2024 年 6 月第 1 版
印　　次　2024 年 6 月第 1 次印刷
书　　号　ISBN 978-7-5720-2673-7/G·2354
定　　价　62.00 元

如发现质量问题，读者可向本社调换　电话：021 - 64373213